the new wealth of nations

the new wealth of nations

taxing cyberspace

arthur j. cordell
t. ran ide

luc soete
& karin kamp

introduction by
mike mccracken

between the lines
Toronto, Canada

© Between The Lines, 1997

Published by
Between The Lines
720 Bathurst Street, #404
Toronto, Ontario
M5S 2R4
Canada

Cover and interior design by
David Vereschagin, Quadrat Communications
Printed in Canada

All rights reserved. No part of this publication may be reproduced, stored in a retrieval system, or transmitted in any form by any means, electronic, mechanical, photocopying, recording, or otherwise, except as may be expressly permitted in writing by the publisher, or CAN-COPY, (photocopying only), 6 Adelaide Street East, Suite 900, Toronto, Ontario, M5C 1H6.

Between The Lines gratefully acknowledges the support of the Ontario Arts Council, the Canadian Heritage Ministry, and the Canada Council for the Arts for our publishing program.

Canadian Cataloguing-in-Publication Data

Main entry under title:

The new wealth of nations : taxing cyberspace

ISBN 1-896357-10-5

1. Wide area networks industry - Taxation - Canada.
I. Ide, Ran.

HE7647.N49 1997   336.2'783843'0971   C97-930266-8

contents

About the contributors vii
Dedication ix

Chapter one 1
Introduction
Perspectives on a bit tax
  Mike McCracken

Chapter two 20
The new wealth of nations
Taxing cyberspace
  Arthur J. Cordell and T. Ran Ide

Chapter three 83
The bit tax
Taxing value in the emerging information society
  Luc Soete and Karin Kamp

about the contributors

Arthur Cordell is a special advisor on information technology policy with Industry Canada and a co-author, with Ran Ide, of *Shifting Time: Social Policy and the Future of Work*. He holds a Ph.D. in economics from Cornell University and is a Fellow of the World Academy of Art and Science.

T. Ran Ide was an educator, broadcast executive, and the founder of TVOntario. During his life he was made an officer of the Order of Canada, and was a member of the Science Council of Canada and the Club of Rome.

Luc Soete and Karin Kamp are associates of the Maastricht Economic Research Institute on Innovation and Technology (MERIT) at the University of Maastricht, the Netherlands. Luc Soete was the chairman of the High Level Expert Group established by the European Commission to advise on the societal aspects of the information society.

Mike McCracken is Chairman and C.E.O. of Informetrica Limited, an Ottawa-based economic research and information company. He is a frequent contributor to the public debate on economic policy, the future of work, and the long-term economic outlook.

dedication

This book is dedicated to Thomas Ranald Ide, affectionately known as Ran.

Ran's illness leading to his death at age 77 on 23 October 1996, slowed him physically but seemed to stimulate his mental acuity. Ran had a restless intelligence that was aimed at understanding why things worked the way they did. Ran's values and core philosophy pushed him beyond merely understanding: he tried to make institutions work better, he tried to figure out ways in which technologies could be used to enhance the common good. His enthusiasm and energy were contagious to students and colleagues alike.

Ran had a strong belief that, as he put it, society is in a race between education and catastrophe. Our work on the ideas in this book was originally stimulated by a quest to understand the implications of information technology for society – in particular the future of work and working; the quality and quantity of jobs.

Having satisfied ourselves that the transition to the "New Economy" would be longer and bumpier than most political leaders were willing to admit, we sought to propose a way to get an income to those who were no longer employable in conventional jobs.

Threats to income, to family, and to the future have, over time, usually led to a "bad" outcome. Ran's preoccupation was that a society marked by disparity, a society of rich and poor with a vanishing middle-class, would be one that could not maintain the conditions for democracy. Thus, he was determined to devise a way to get at the productivity of information technology so that a more equitable distribution of the wealth created by this technology could be achieved.

The suggestions contained in this book mark one such way.

Other approaches will, I am sure, be proposed over time. Something must be done to protect the hard-won gains of economic development achieved by working Canadians.

Ran's career was in education and public service. He was a teacher, principal, school inspector, and administrator. He was the creator of educational television in Ontario and twice honoured with the LL.D. (Queen's and Waterloo universities). Ran was an officer of the Order of Canada, and a member of the Science Council of Canada and the Club of Rome. He was a Fellow of the World Academy of Art and Science, the Ontario Institute for Studies in Education (OISE), and the Ontario Teacher's Federation (OTF).

Above all, Ran was a colleague, friend, and role model.

The reader should see this book, *The New Wealth of Nations*, as part of Ran's public service legacy – as Ran's parting educational gift.

Arthur J. Cordell
Ottawa, January, 1997

one
introduction
perspectives on a bit tax

mike mccracken

Change, we are told as we approach the millennium, is the only constant. The world of work is being transformed, in good part because of computers, communications, and related enabling technologies. The economy seems to be working in contradictory ways, with growth and productivity rising at the same time that unemployment seems to be a growing concern. Governments claim that they are impotent in the face of globalization, with politics (and an anxious electorate) becoming more volatile as old certainties fade away.

Yet there appears to be little new thinking, despite the magnitude of change in the so-called "New Economy." The names of some of the schools of economic thought might suggest "new" or fresh ideas: neo-conservative (or neoclassical), neo-Keynesian, neo-Malthusian. But the second half of the word is the operative one, with little emerging about new goals, new tools, or even a new consensus on how the world is working. As a result, most discussions of policy don't go very far.

When another group shows up (what I call the "technologists"), they seem to attract an inordinate amount of attention. Witness the recent success of Jeremy Rifkin's provocatively titled book, *The End of Work*.[1] Ran Ide's and Arthur Cordell's ideas fit in here. They have both identified and elaborated the new wealth of nations, and have developed innovative proposals for new tax bases. They address the challenge of how to transfer incomes directly from the source that is thought to be pushing people out of jobs to those in need.

Their proposal for an "information technology tax" or "bit tax" will no doubt be controversial.[2] Will it be politically acceptable? Would its application help to improve the economic prospects for the unemployed? We do not know. But if we reject such proposals without careful consideration, it will be at our own peril.

In a world with increasing uses of information technology within each country and between countries, it is not surprising that attention has turned to the role of information technology in the economy. In particular, there is growing debate about whether such technologies are creating or destroying jobs, improving productivity, and enhancing or reducing the quality of life. At the same time, income from paid work seems to be under strain in almost all the developed countries, as high unemployment, declining real wage rates, or a combination of these factors erodes real earned incomes. Governments find traditional revenues from labour income growing more slowly. One obvious option is to raise tax rates on labour income (e.g., through payroll taxes and personal income taxes). But this is contrary to the desire to promote employment and to gain the political endorsement of those working – and voting.

The fundamental problem is that there is no agreement on the underlying economic situation, the mechanisms at work within it, and the driving forces determining the future course of economic development. Perceptions differ. This has been expressed by Kenneth Boulding[3] as the problem of different "images." More recently, Robert Heilbroner used the notion of "vision," or, as he puts it, "the all-important terrain over which intellectual contest is waged in political and sociological controversy."[4] His point is that there is no shared vision among mainstream economists at the present time, which leaves them increasingly irrelevant to the public policy debate. But the problem may be that there are too many different views and little understanding of the reasons for the differences.

Perspectives on where we are trying to go

In the sections below several distinct "schools" are described, with what I hope are clear statements of the objectives for economic policy that they each favour, the mechanisms in the economy that they believe are at work, and the implicit scenarios for the future that are contained in their policy prescriptions.

These schools of thought and their usual labels and proponents include:

- neoconservative, Reform, Conservative, Liberal, neoclassical, Department of Finance and Bank of Canada, OECD;
- neo-Keynesian, NDP, the former Economic Council of Canada, CLC, Alternative Budget group, ILO;
- neo-Malthusians, Club of Rome, sustainability, "Greens," some environmental groups; and
- technologists, Jeremy Rifkin, John Stuart Mill's longer-term "Steady State."

One way of distinguishing among the groups is to consider their view on a specific policy objective, like "full employment." This device is used below, given the sharp differences of opinion about labour markets. Each section is written as if a reporter had asked one of the gurus of the group for a quick overview of current economic objectives, with special emphasis on "the jobs issue," the planned policy settings, and the likely course of economic developments in the coming decade.

Little distance, little time – neoconservatives

The headline is: Current policies on track, continuing improvement expected.

Objectives

"Full Employment," or the "natural" rate of unemployment, or NAIRU (the non-accelerating inflation rate of unemployment) is currently about 8 or 9 per cent in Canada. The economy is approaching this level, so no special stimulus is needed. Growth is achieved through private investment and private consumption. Government's role is to maintain the price stability achieved so far and to keep the inflation rate moving lower. At the same time, it is also important for governments to reduce their deficits.

Policy mechanisms and settings

The maintenance of price stability will result in a major improvement in business confidence, private sector investment, and an acceleration of technological change. In turn this will improve our international competitiveness, which will generate private sector jobs and increase real wages.

Structural policies have also been implemented that bolster business confidence, remove distortions in or of relative prices, and move the fiscal balances of government towards longer-term structural surpluses. These structural policies include:

- NAFTA and FTA (remove distortionary tariffs and improve access to markets);
- GST (removes uneven taxation between services and manufactured goods);
- reduction in the size of government (cutbacks in employment, services, and involvement);
- reform of the UI system (fewer beneficiaries as percentage of unemployed, no benefits to voluntary quits, more time to qualify, shorter duration – all of which increase workforce mobility and flexibility);
- minimum wage reform (reductions in real wage);
- deregulation (transport, finance, energy); and
- privatization (air and rail transportation, oil and gas).

And more changes are planned. These include:

- further deregulation (communications and finance);
- privatization (highways, sewage treatment, government operations, prisons, social housing, electricity generation and distribution);

- less emphasis on regional development;
- removal of internal barriers to trade;
- welfare reform (removal of incentives for people to stay on welfare);
- education financing reform (introduction of higher tuition); and
- health care reform (forced rebalancing of services across components and use of queuing as rationing device).

All of these structural changes are expected to further reduce the size and role of governments, thereby fostering further improvements in business confidence with consequent benefits.

The other mechanism is the linkage between real interest rates and government debts/deficits. When the debt ratio starts to fall, real interest rates will decline. This will further stimulate business investment, consumer spending, and housing starts, while relieving some of the pressure on government deficits from high interest payments. Indeed, a virtuous circle will emerge, in which debt ratio declines will lower real interest rates, which in turn will lower debt ratios again.

Scenario for the next decade

It has taken some time to reduce inflationary expectations, to set the fiscal house in order, and to implement the structural changes. Over the next ten years we will reap the benefits of these changes with little additional need for intervention by government. Indeed, if the role of government can be further reduced, this will just help reinforce the trend and provide the room for the private sector to expand.

Unemployment will move down to NAIRU. We may find that NAIRU has shifted downward as a result of the structural changes to UI and the further erosion of minimum wages. If so, when we get there we may try to reduce it slowly below the 8–9 per cent range. The debt ratio will start falling with increased rapidity as the decade unfolds. This will ease real interest rates, which will help reinvigorate the economy. Government policy will focus on completing the structural reforms affecting markets, as well as working on old-age income, education, and health issues.

Any attempt to implement short-term policies aimed at creating employment will do more harm than good, by destroying business confidence and upsetting international and domestic financial markets.

Excess demand inflation is always just around the corner. Even though it was last seen in the mid-1970s along with an international supply-side shock on oil and other commodities, it was thought to have reappeared in the early 1980s, and again, at least in Toronto, during the late 1980s. The appearance coincided with the unemployment rate falling below 8 per cent. Hence we know what NAIRU is.

Fiscal restraint in the form of expenditure cuts or tax increases does not really affect people. They simply adjust their expectations about future taxes and anticipate lower real interest rates (Barro/Lucas effect). Distortions in or of relative prices are mainly the result of government actions through regulations, taxes, and subsidies.

A long way and it has been a long time – neo-Keynesians

The headline is: The current situation is unsatisfactory and current policies will result in further deterioration.

Objectives

The economy is some distance from full employment, defined as a situation in which everyone who wants to work can do so. There may be some frictional unemployment as people move between jobs, but the level of unemployment at full employment would be at or below 3 per cent. With the current rate at about 10 per cent, there is much distance to travel. If economic growth is to be the device used to close the gap, then we need real economic growth of an additional 14 to 18 per cent, on top of the potential growth rate of 2.5 to 3 per cent per year required to sustain the unemployment rate at any level by accommodating net new entrants into the labour force and the annual productivity increases. Since the participation rate has declined since 1989, it may be the case that strong growth will lead to an unusually large increase in labour force growth, requiring even more additional growth than stipulated.

The objective of full employment should result in a substantial improvement in real disposable income, as a result of increased employment, higher real wages with tighter labour markets, and lower taxes through reduced expenditures required to support the UI, welfare, and other social costs of high unemployment.

Policy mechanisms and settings

The fundamental challenge to be overcome is the lack of effective demand. This requires a major reversal of current policy settings, with the adoption of a stimulative fiscal and monetary policy. Lower real interest rates may trigger a lower exchange rate. This will be helpful in the medium term since it will promote exports and import-competing industries. Lower interest rates will also help to stimulate investment by business and in housing, as well as consumer durables.

Fiscal pressures on government will be helped by lower interest rates and by a recovering economy. Some "pump-priming" now can help to build consumer and business confidence, which will lead to increased spending and hiring.

Structural policy changes have resulted in major adverse shocks to many businesses, resulting in lower employment, lack of confidence, and postponement in investment decisions. Restoration of business confidence requires leadership by government in promoting further growth, increased sales of domestically produced goods and services, and lower interest rates. Nothing else will work.

Productivity growth is always welcome, particularly when it is shared among the sectors through higher real wages and lower prices. Increases are more likely to occur when investment picks up and when economic growth is rapid. In such an environment everyone helps put in place the necessary adjustments to achieve major productivity gains. This contrasts with the behaviour under slow growth, where fear of losing jobs makes adjustment more difficult.

High real interest rates and slow growth have been the

principal causes of rising debt ratios for governments. Significantly lower real interest rates and higher growth will reverse this rise, even if there is a temporary increase in primary deficits and inflation as a result of deliberate stimulus.

Scenario for the next decade

Real economic growth of 4 to 5 per cent per year should be the target for the next decade. Business investment will be strong since demand will be increasing substantially. The unemployment rate should decline by at least one percentage point per year in the first part of the decade, with possibly a slightly slower pace towards the end. The objective is 3 per cent nationally, although this may mean slightly higher rates in Atlantic Canada and very low rates in the West.

Inflation is not expected to be a problem, although it may be higher than current targets. The focus will be on inflation in Canada remaining at or below U.S. inflation rates, since it is our major trading partner. If a problem emerges, then we will look at other income policies instead of using higher unemployment rates for controlling nominal income growth and inflation.

Government deficits will not balloon since economic growth and lower interest rates will offset the fiscal stimulus and economic growth will increase the denominator in the debt ratios.

Underlying Assumptions

High real interest rates and slow growth have been the culprits leading to rising debt ratios. Lower rates will reverse that situation. An increase in income inequality has been a result of the higher real interest rates and slow growth as well, coupled with the loss of low-skill, blue-collar manufacturing sector employment and the growing gap in earning power between knowledge-based workers and others. This has exacerbated the problem of lack of effective demand and has eroded consumer confidence.

External trade is limited in its capacity to pull the economy along. If we run too large a surplus, our trading partners will ask us to limit our use of that avenue, or face possible trade sanctions. Distortions to relative prices and markets arise from many sources, including oligopolies, information gaps, and other forms of market failures. Externalities also may require major adjustments to market prices in order that they reflect full social costs. Regulation and improved information are key roles for government in ensuring "good" markets.

Structural adjustments to the economy, such as NAFTA and FTA, should be helped along by governments rather than ignored or made worse by inappropriate macroeconomic policies.

We face major environmental constraints – neo-Malthusians

The headline is: Enough is enough! Now is the time to get serious about the environment.

Canada is among the richest nations in the world, measured either as assets per capita or in terms of annual income per household. It has translated some of this wealth into a decent infrastructure, a good health system, and an advanced education system. Indeed, that is why Canada continues to rank among the top countries in the Human Development Index.[5]

Objectives

The time has come to stop growing, both absolutely and in per capita use of resources and production of wastes. For example, it is necessary for Canada (and the other rich developed countries) to start by reducing GHG (greenhouse gas) emissions by 25 per cent. This will require a redistribution of activities away from energy using and waste producing to energy saving and reusing and recycling of materials. It is expected that it should be possible to achieve the required emission reduction without experiencing an absolute decline in GDP, although that is a challenge.

The central problem is the lack of capacity in the world to absorb the environmental damage being done currently and to continue to sustain life, even at current levels of resource use. The warning signals are increasing, including the recent news about declines in fertility for men and women, linked to industrial chemicals in the biosystem.

Policy mechanisms and settings

The emphasis of policy will be on getting the "signals" right by applying various specific taxes to resources for which demand needs to be reduced. In particular, carbon taxes will be a major part of the strategy for recycling carbon tax revenues through directed investments in energy-conserving activities.

Reduction of population growth, both in Canada and elsewhere, will become a more important objective. The likely effect in Canada will be to reduce immigration substantially, since it now accounts for over half of all population growth.

The plight of individuals will be responded to by income redistribution through tax and transfer policies and the redistribution of work. Lower real interest rates are part of the adjustment, mainly to ensure that all groups participate in the adjustment.

Scenario for the next decade

Economic growth will slow to zero and measured unemployment will rise substantially, unless work is shared (see below). Higher taxes on energy and other resources will reduce incomes and employment in the energy-using sectors. The focus of public attention will be on progress made in reducing GHG emissions and other environmental indicators, not on GDP growth or the unemployment rate.

Underlying assumptions

Reductions in GHG can be achieved without actually stopping the production of some commodities, either by process changes or recycling. The public will respond to an urgent requirement to move to a sustainable lifestyle. Revenues raised from environmental taxes can be recycled into the economy without promoting energy use elsewhere.

Technology will save us from work – technologists

The headlines are: More downsizing frees up another group of workers! Average workweek approaches 20 hours.

Some would view the developments of the last two decades as the beginning or dawning of a new age, which will be characterized by the reduced need for people to work, even as the outputs from the factories and offices grow. Technology in the forms of computers, communications, numerically controlled tools, new life forms, and other innovations will enable all of us to work much less, without giving up any consumption. The policy focus becomes one of distribution of buying power rather than one of increasing production.

The label "technologists" includes both optimists and pessimists, both agreeing on the labour-displacing forces, but of differing views on the ability of our society to restructure itself to distribute incomes in a form that will be acceptable to the majority while taking care of the minorities.

Objectives

The economic indicators of public concern are no longer the unemployment rate and the employment ratio. Rather, the focus is on real disposable income per household, including both private incomes and consumption of goods and services provided by the state (health, education, training, culture, etc.). Distribution of this broad form of income is also important, with various indicators of the distribution (poverty levels, ratio of top 20 per cent to bottom 20 per cent, etc.) being used to monitor progress.

But economic indicators are only part of the story. Social indicators such as life expectancy, literacy, education levels, youth suicides, environmental quality, and voter participation also receive increased attention, from the media, politicians, and citizens.

An increased emphasis is placed on community sustainability, family values, and the maintenance of own values – for all groups – as part of the broad notion of "quality of life."

Policy mechanisms and settings

Government actions are key to the redistribution of income, both through transfers and by encouraging families to acquire claims on the profits of Canadian-based enterprises. Taxes that rely on wage income must be shifted to growing bases, in particular the value added by enterprises operating in Canada, including those producing for export.

Lower interest rates will help to redistribute income from the creditors to the debtors, although with increasing reliance on property income, real interest rates should not be allowed to go negative. Indeed, if the desire is to redistribute wealth, various wealth taxes would be a more appropriate device.

With major income redistribution, immigration is likely to

become tighter, since the shared cost implied is much higher. As well, citizenship and evidence of active participation in society may become necessary attributes to qualify for income transfers.

Scenario for the next decade

The fear of change is a major inhibiting factor in adopting new practices in both the workplace and governments. But rising discontent will push for change. Experiments will begin with "social wages" being paid to people willing to work for non-profit agencies delivering services in the community, including child care, care for the elderly, health promotion, education, etc. Although such incomes will be taxable, the amounts will be low enough for most that it will not be of consequence.

Reduction in the workweek to a four-day week or equivalent practices will become standard in governments and will spread to large employers in the private sector by the end of the decade. At the same time, downsizing will no longer be seen as a threat if an organization adopts a strategy for dealing with it.

An inheritance and gift tax will be introduced immediately after the election of 2001, with the funds notionally "earmarked" for redistribution to lower-income citizens. The debate will be about whether there should be a "lump-sum" transfer to people or an ongoing income flow, equivalent to what the wealth transfer would earn.

Immigration will be limited to 100,000 net per year, from 2001 on. All landed immigrants will be expected to "normalize" their status within five years, or at least before qualifying for an income transfer. By 2005, a GAI or Guaranteed Annual Income will emerge, combining Employment Insurance, social assistance, seniors' pensions, child allowances, etc., into one system of payment. The monthly payments will be sensitive to the family makeup, income from other sources, and age of the recipient, with a full tax-back by the time average income is reached.

Working-time scenarios for the next decade

For ease of reference, the scenarios have been "coloured" appropriately. "Purple" is a combination of "red" and "blue," the colours of the Canadian Liberal and Conservative parties, and a shorthand for the status quo. "Orange" is one of the colours of the New Democratic Party, the closest we have to a party concerned with full employment and with a view that there is a positive role for government in society. "Green" is the colour associated with the environmental movement, although it has yet to organize in Canada along political party lines. And "sunshine" connotes all the colours in the rainbow (a synthesis), or the "light at the end of the tunnel" (the future).

Purple (red and blue)

With the desire for more deregulation and the emphasis on maintaining international competitiveness, the only changes in hours of work will be those arrived at voluntarily between employers and employees. The notion of "flexibility" will be interpreted primarily as an employer need for "just-in-time" people, multiple shifts, and maximum overtime, preferably without a premium for such work. The underlying premise is that the value of workers' leisure time for employers is essentially zero and any value to the employee is not of concern to the employer (or government). The high fixed costs per employee dictate the desire to minimize the number of employees.

Orange

The likelihood of closing the output gap through macroeconomic policies is small in the next decade. A substantial reduction in the working time of existing workers by 10 or 20 per cent could significantly reduce unemployment, improve the bargaining power of labour, and provide increased leisure time to those most likely to value it highly – those who are now working and have incomes. With expected productivity improvements of half of the reduction, it is possible to provide increased real wages per hour while reducing the total number of hours worked per person employed.

Green

There is a need to move away from the "consumer" society to the "conserver" society, with less emphasis on what we produce and more on our lifestyle. Adoption of "voluntary simplicity" by an increasing number of well-off people is but an example of this trend.

Sunshine

Contemplation, physical exercise (cycling), recycling, and other "good" activities should replace our energy-using, wasteful undertakings. With less need for monetary income, it should be easy to work fewer hours for pay and to spend more time on community and family activities as part of a general rebalancing of human activity.

Indeed, the reduction of working time should be seen as a positive sign that we have finally reached John Stuart Mill's "Steady State" in which our needs are met with increasingly less time required to achieve them.

Bit tax scenarios for the next decade

In the policy settings and scenarios above only passing mention is made of a "bit tax" as part of the solution. In this section we examine the likely role and attitudes towards the introduction of a new tax base under each of the scenarios.

Purple (red and blue)

There is strong resistance to any new tax by both the "red" and "blue" factions. Partly this flows from the belief that everything to date has been "right" and therefore needs no changes, just patience. With a desire to reduce the size and role of government in society, quite popular within this group, tax reductions are the order of the day, when the fiscal measures of performance (debt ratios) improve.

A bit tax will only emerge if other countries adopt such a tax, or if a strong political following emerges elsewhere, suggesting that the tax might be "copied" for political benefit.

Orange

A bit tax is a possible replacement for payroll taxes as part of a more general reform of the tax structure. In a world with high unemployment, taxing labour services less, and those activities that are replacing labour more, has a certain logic to it. But such a shift in mix alone is unlikely to result in a fully employed economy. This will only come about with significantly lower interest rates and increased spending, fueled either by deficit financing or a reduction of savings of persons or businesses.

Green

The environmentalists are most concerned with altering behaviour through environmental taxes. By taxing resource use more, they hope to discourage it. If they can also redirect the revenues to activities that have beneficial environmental effects so much the better. To the extent that most information technology (IT) is seen as environmentally benign, then it is not part of the their future tax base.

Sunshine

In a world with less paid work, there will be a need for new revenue sources for governments in order to support substantial income or wealth redistribution. Another option is a substantial redistribution of the ownership of production among the population, although even this option involves a transition period and some mechanisms to provide for new entrants to society.

A bit tax will be part of future tax bases, along with the Tobin Tax,[6] wealth taxes, and other distributional taxes. Indeed, much might be learned from the application of a Tobin tax on financial transactions, even though the purposes are rather different. Indeed, the bit tax is primarily for revenue generation, not for the reduction in the flows of information. The Tobin tax in its original form was designed to reduce exchange rate volatility by making a very short-term transaction relatively expensive. Only more recently has it become a focal point for providing alternative financing for international development and institutions. This latter need has been driven by the continuing reductions of foreign aid and the withholding of defined contributions to international organizations by some countries in order to increase their influence above that provided in the charters.

In the sunshine scenario, there is a bit tax applied in Canada through its information intermediaries (e.g., phone companies, Internet suppliers, cable systems, etc.). Similar taxes are imposed in other countries in the world, since the lack of paid work is not unique. This multiple-country approach has greatly reduced the costs of ensuring compliance, even though the rates do differ somewhat across regions.

Robust steps

At this time we do not know which scenario will come to dominate the future. But we can ask a simple question. Are there some things that could be done that would be appropriate under most or all scenarios? Such steps can be described as being "robust," or equally positive under any scenario.

Macroeconomic policy changes

The prescription is well-known although not taken recently. Ease up on real interest rates, ease up on fiscal restraint, and focus on reducing the unemployment rate. Whatever progress can be made here will make the transition to the future much easier.

Now is the time to talk about "income policies," not in the narrow sense of how to control union wages, but rather in the broad context of how incomes are to be generated and shared in the future under many different scenarios. It will take some time to put in place institutions that can be trusted by all parties in this area.

Introduce a modest telecommunications tax

Start with a 5 per cent tax on the gross revenue of telecommunication companies and other information intermediaries. This would raise a modest $1–2 billion per year, sufficient to make the collection overhead modest relative to the income, but not so large that major behavioural responses by either the customers or the suppliers are likely to be important. The companies paying the tax initially would be allowed, indeed encouraged, by regulatory authorities to pass the tax on in their output prices. The interests of the company and of the government will coincide; both want the tax applied in a manner that minimizes distortions and disincentive effects as much as possible.

Although about two-thirds of telecommunication revenues arise from purchases by other industries, it should be clear that "cascading" of the tax is not really a problem. While information transmitted (and taxed) may be retransmitted at a later time or to a different place, there inevitably will be some change (compression or blending) that makes the information a new product or service.

The revenue collected should be recycled into the economy,

preferably with a focus on providing social employment for those otherwise unemployable. At the same time, there should be an information-gathering framework put in place, both on the tax side (e.g., number of bytes being transferred by various groups) and on the benefits side (e.g., where are those technologically unemployed best re-engaged in society?).

Voluntary actions on working time

Adjustments in working time that occur as a result of employer-employee arrangements and conform to the labour codes are to be encouraged, if they result in fewer hours of work per year.

Some firms are becoming "doughnut" or "shamrock" organizations that increasingly use non-standard workers (part-time, contract, temporary) or contract out activities previously done internally. At the same time people are becoming self-employed, with few or no employees. These changes introduce the potential for changes in working time by breaking down the dominance of "employees at standard hours." Policies that make such changes easier for the people involved, including their continuing participation in social programs, pensions systems, and training activities, would be robust policies.

Some of the "right things" with working-time consequences include[7]:

- availability of unpaid family leave to all workers;
- encouragement of flexible hours and time;
- encouragement of phased-in retirement;
- encouragement of students to stay in school longer;
- reduction of long hours;
- training sabbaticals promoted as a way of using up compensatory time or of reducing working time;
- enforcement of labour standards that currently exist; and
- adoption of similar standards across regions by upgrading those that lengthen working time.

Changing perspectives

If we are to deal realistically with the transformation of the economy – and society – a shift in values and institutions is necessary. Part of the change will require a shared vision of how we want society to work. This will not flow from traditional institutions alone, be they government, business, or labour. Rather, I suspect, the new ideas will have their origins in many conversations among citizens.

The time is now to come to terms with working time and to recognize, as Stephen Leacock did in 1920, that:

> The nerves of our industrial civilization are worn thin with the rattle of its own machinery. The industrial world is restless, over-strained, and quarrelsome It seethes with furious discontent, and looks about it eagerly for a fight. It needs a rest. It should be sent, as nerve patients are, to the seaside or the quiet of the hills. Failing this, it should at least slacken the pace of its work and shorten its working day. And for this the thing needed is an altered public opinion on the subject of work in relation to human character and development.[8]

This book is an excellent starting point. New ideas, put forward provocatively, can stimulate real change. The concept of taxing technology to maintain society should start many conversations! As you read this book ask yourself the following questions:
- What do you see as a desirable society for your children to grow up in?
- Is there a difference between "working" and "work"?
- Should the expression "full employment" become "full engagement"?
- Is a full-time job really the most desirable option?
- Is a job "the measure" of someone's contribution to society?
- Is a job the only satisfactory way to deliver income to people?
- Does taxing wage income make sense in a world of high unemployment?
- Has information become the major resource in a modern economy?

Answers to these questions – and the ideas in this book – are fundamental if we are to at last emerge from the deep freeze that has so far paralyzed discussions of the future.

Notes

1. Jeremy Rifkin, *The End of Work: The Decline of the Global Labor Force and the Dawn of the Post-market Era* (New York: G.P. Putnam's Sons, 1995).
2. Mike McCracken, editor, *The Search for New Tax Bases for the 21st Century* (Informetrica Limited, 1995).
3. Kenneth Boulding, *The Image*, (Ann Arbor: University of Michigan Press, 1956).
4. Robert Heilbroner and William Milberg, *The Crisis of Vision in Modern Economic Thought*, (Cambridge: Cambridge University Press, 1995), p.4.
5. UNDP, *Human Development Report 1996* (New York: Oxford University Press, 1996), p.28.
6. Mahbub ul Haq, Inge Kaul, and Isabelle Grunberg, *The Tobin Tax: Coping with Financial Volatility*, (New York: Oxford University Press, 1996).
7. Further recommendations are contained in the *Report of the Advisory Group on Working Time and the Distribution of Work* (Ottawa: Human Resources and Development Canada, 1994) .
8. Stephen Leacock (1920), "The Unsolved Riddle of Social Justice," in *Social Criticism*, ed. Alan Bowker (Toronto: University of Toronto Press, 1996), p.143.

two
the new wealth of nations
taxing cyberspace

arthur j. cordell & t. ran ide

The challenge

Two prominent twentieth-century economists, recently writing about Adam Smith and his 1776 masterpiece *The Wealth of Nations*, have described his book as "The most successful not only of all books on economics but, with the possible exception of Darwin's *Origin of Species*, of all scientific books that have appeared to this day" and "A work that one contemplates with awe."[1] The book has become one of the classics of economic literature and Smith has been called the earliest writer to properly define the nature of capitalism. Underlying Smith's work was a belief that self-interest and natural liberty are the two principles that contribute to the wealth of nations and to the annual labour that originally supplies it "with all the necessities and conveniences of life."

Although it is difficult to argue the validity of these principles, why, then, do we speak of "the *new* wealth of nations"? Because Smith and the other classical economists who followed him quite properly applied their analysis and ideas to an industrial system based on factory-like establishments and the division of labour. Today, however, information and communications technology (ICT) is shifting the economic ground on which we stand. Theories and policies that functioned well in an industrial era now seem dysfunctional in the information age. What we are witnessing is, in effect, a transformation in the nature of work that has literally changed the form and substance of the society of which we are a part.

This metamorphosis is such that the very nature of the annual labour to which Smith referred requires a new appraisal. We need to determine what comprises the wealth of nations today and how that wealth is distributed when the fruits of production are more ephemeral than those of the past. We need to better understand how technology is affecting production and consumption so we can prepare for a different world of work and working.

New tools have always been developed to make the work of the labourer more productive and thereby to reduce the cost of production. In theory, the end result is twofold: the price of the goods in question is lowered and there is additional social income available to spend on more products or new goods and services. This is the heart of economic growth: greater productivity leads to lowered prices that translate to an increase in real incomes, thus creating more investment, more existing goods, and new products.

Up to a point this has proved to be true. As labour was replaced in the primary industries such as agriculture, opportunities were being created in the growing manufacturing sector. As new tools replaced jobs in the factories, a burgeoning service sector provided a profusion of new openings for those displaced. But then, as people in the service sector began to be replaced by automated switching systems, automatic tellers, electronic funds transfer systems, data exchanges, et cetera, the only sector that seemed to be open to the newly unemployed appeared to be welfare, with all the difficulties, both economic and psychological, that such a change implies.

The problems facing society today are huge. Even when the profit and loss picture for corporations seems to be brighter, the outlook for workers remains bleak. Globalization, sparked by the ease with which money and management structures can be moved, is threatening traditional forms of governance based on the sovereignty of the nation-state. The planned economies of the socialist world are largely bankrupt and free market systems seem headed for a major adjustment.

The underlying problem is a human one. It is unthinkable to imagine a society where twenty to thirty per cent of young people are unable to find jobs, with the majority of the remainder required to accept part-time and low-paying work.[2] Downsizing has reached into the very core of modern business, with many middle managers finding themselves "on the street" while still in the prime of life. As one writer pointed out when discussing the nature of crises that beset parliamentary democracies, "the most basic concerns are about working and making a living, about the security of person and property, about the stability in public and private life that allows one to plan for the day after tomorrow and not just from day to day."[3] These are the issues that have to be faced, and they require that the new wealth flowing from information technologies be rigorously examined to see whether that wealth is being distributed widely and wisely.

The irony is that the world in general is not in a state where there are no jobs to be done; rather, the world is plagued with insolvent governments. The need for work related to the environment, the resolution of the problem of poverty, and the care of an increasing number of old and helpless people has never been greater.

The problem does not lie with our ability to produce. The new tools provided by microelectronics and sophisticated communications technologies provide us with the ability to solve almost all of our economic problems. Ideally, the 1990s ought to be the best of times. The new technologies bring important benefits. The machine control features affect production processes through the use of robots, computer-assisted design, and systems engineering. These mechanisms are clean, highly efficient, and productive. The goods turned out are more cheaply made and require little of the monotonous and back-breaking labour so characteristic of the past.

As productivity increases, so does wealth; as technologies become less polluting, the ecosystem improves; as access to information becomes easier, knowledge increases. The ability of the human race to make better value judgments ought to follow.

While much of the productivity from ICT is recorded in lower prices or in higher profits or salaries, some of it disappears into the networks and is not measured in the traditional GNP statistics. Like many social benefits, such as volunteer work and homemaking, this aspect of productivity is considered apart from the economy and is reflected neither in wages nor in capital. If some productivity flowing from ICT is not captured by labour, capital, or taxes, then our society is, in effect, not consuming all the new wealth produced by the new technologies: we are poorer than we ought to be. *The Economist Survey*, "The World Economy," September 1996, suggests that the prime reason why productivity is not as high as it might be is because "(t)he tools used for measuring productivity are more suited to the output of 19th century dark satanic mills than 21st century electronic wizardry." The productivity is being produced by ICT; by neither measuring it accurately nor fully appropriating it for public or private uses, society is poorer than it ought to be.

The challenge is to ensure full access to the new wealth of nations and to use it for socially desirable ends. The question is how. We intend to address these issues by going back to basics and looking at the factors of production to see how relevant they are in the world of today. We will look at the new technologies from the standpoint of their inherent advantages, and see whether some of the growing disparities in income and opportunities could be caused by them. The elements that contribute to the quality of life will be examined with the view of determining to what degree modern-day practices have affected them and to what extent current inequities have influenced the distribution of wealth and the resulting deficiency in consumer demand. The trend to a global marketplace will also be considered, as will the associated advantages and disadvantages to globalization. Finally we will examine the current revenue crunch faced by the industrialized states, review the tax policies of the past to determine their relevance in the age of information, and propose alternatives to approaches that appear to us to be outmoded. We intend to conclude with what we believe are solutions to the current problems and discuss, in some detail, our proposals.

Factors of production

In some ways economics has always been with us. The word economics is derived from the ancient Greek word *oikonomia*. This roughly translates to mean household management. An important function of the housekeeper is to ensure that food, clothing, and shelter are in place and of sufficient quantities, and that the various household tasks are done to ensure that the household is kept running. The ancient Greeks used *oikonomia* to refer to the organizing of activities of the household and to larger political units as well, such as the city-state. *Oikonomia*, as used in ancient times, can be thought of as an early image or idea of production.

In one way or another, societies have always produced, traded, consumed, and distributed products and services. Over the years the reasons why societies produced in one way or another, were wealthier at one time or another, or wealthier than their neighbours, have varied. Along with production and how things get produced have come theories of distribution. Who gets the product? How does the wealth of the nation get distributed?

Through the ages various theories regarding the wealth of nations were advanced. How and why do nations prosper? Why is one nation wealthy while others are not? Why is one nation wealthy at one period of time while years later it is suddenly in poverty? Much thought and study have been given to the root causes of wealth.

Economics and human activity are intimately related. The economy does not exist in a vacuum. The early notions of wealth arose from a study of those activities that seemed to lead to an increase in wealth and well-being, both for the nation-state and for the population at large.

An early set of ideas concerning the theory of wealth has come to be called Mercantilism. Popular in the seventeenth and eighteenth centuries, it did not rest on an elaborate theory; rather, it was the set of actions and ideas practised by politicians, statesmen, and merchants. In essence, Mercantilism was based on the belief that the best policy for a nation was the same as that for an individual merchant. By selling for more than the purchase price, the wealth of the firm would be increased. So too, its advocates believed, would the wealth of nations. Thus the wealthier nation would be the one that is the "better" trader; the one that sells more than it buys; the one that exports more than it imports. To this end, tariffs were advocated to obtain a favourable balance of trade.

Unemployment was not seen as a problem since the availability of labour would drive down wages. Lower wages, in turn, would lead to low-cost production, thereby increasing the possibility for exports. The intent was always to provide a favourable balance of trade for the home country. A favourable balance of trade, after all, was the source of wealth.

Reacting to Mercantilism were a group of eighteenth-century thinkers in France known as the Physiocrats; they believed that wealth lay not in industry or commerce but in the land itself. Physiocracy, or "the rule of nature," arose from a concept of natural law. All wealth, they claimed, ultimately derived from the land, according to a natural law that is both basic and benevolent. Without food and fibres, wood, minerals, and stone, organized society would founder. Wealth could not exist. For Physiocrats, those who worked the land were the only true producers of wealth. Industrialists, traders, and craftsmen were "sterile." The only surpluses, the only wealth, came from agricultural activities. Since the only surpluses came from the land, all other workers could share in the bounty of land as payment for their services. But, by definition, the activities of non-agricultural workers, while necessary, were not productive. The Physiocrats thought that, as the only surplus was to be found in the land, the land and its output were the only valid source of taxes. All other taxes, such as excise and import duties, were interferences with the natural order and should be abolished.

The Physiocrats were the inventors of the term "laissez faire." They questioned why national policies should be oriented toward increased trade and exports. Since wealth could only arise from the skilful use of indigenous natural resources, an export surplus amounted to the shipping out of more goods than were received in return. Such a policy could only impoverish farmers, households, and the nation. They believed it would be better to leave the economy to the natural order of things, that is, laissez faire.

Adam Smith went to France and studied Physiocracy. He was impressed with the concept of laissez faire and took up the argument that market forces should be allowed to operate without government intervention. But some ideas seemed at odds with his observations, which were drawn from an economy on the eve of the Industrial Revolution. Smith's epic treatise, *The Wealth of Nations*, focused on production resulting from labour and resources. Wealth could be increased according to the skill and efficiency with which labour is applied and according to the percentage of the population at work. Wealth was measured as total production in relation to the size of the population, or as income per capita.

The key to wealth, he maintained, lay in an increase in production (a function of the division of labour) and in the introduction of machinery. The division of labour could extend as far as the market could be expanded and the larger the market, the greater the division of labour, the greater the output, and hence, the greater the wealth of the nation. Trade resulting from increased production would lead to real wealth accumulation. Nations specializing in those goods that could be produced with the highest quality at the least cost to the producer could and should trade. No nation could gain by making something that it could buy more cheaply elsewhere. In this sense Smith was an early, if not the first, proponent of the value of the global marketplace.

His ideas continue to this day; they are consciously or unconsciously sprinkled in speeches to Chambers of Commerce and are found in introductory lectures in economics virtually everywhere. Building on laissez faire and self-interest, Smith felt that the greatest good for the greatest number would arise by allowing individuals to operate from their self-interest; this could best be achieved by allowing markets everywhere to operate openly and freely. He believed that wealth is created by labour and machinery, and only by increasing growth could wages be increased, since only then could output increase faster than population.

Distribution of the nation's wealth was determined by the theory of the day. According to the Mercantilists, traders would receive the greatest returns; for the Physiocrats, agriculture and resources would generate the greatest returns; for Adam Smith and his followers (now referred to as the classical economists) returns would flow to the productive factors: capital, labour, and land.

Karl Marx also wrote about the wealth of nations. Marx, like many of his predecessors including Smith, believed that the value of commodities is based on the labour expended on them. The price of the product reflects the labour used to make that product. Capitalists buy productive inputs, which are combined with labour to produce the final product, and make a profit. This profit is the spur for production.

Marx referred to profit as surplus value. What is paid to labour by employers is the critical minimum to keep labourers fed and clothed (the iron law of wages). What is collected from the final customer is what represents the true value of the labour. The capitalist appropriates for himself the difference between what is paid to labour and what is received from selling the product in the market. Marx concluded that one of the reasons for business cycles and depressions was that capitalists failed to distribute to labour the full value of its product. This led to production being greater than consumption since labour was underrewarded for its efforts and lacked sufficient money to "clear the market" of all goods produced.

The nineteenth-century British economist John Stuart Mill, like Marx, wondered how society could be made better and how the benefits of progress could be more evenly distributed. Mill's theories represented a fundamental change. He asserted that the distribution of wealth was not governed by unalterable natural law, but could be influenced by the will of man. Mill accepted theories of production, but felt that the distribution of wealth was "a matter of human institution solely." He also broadened the notion of capital beyond money itself to include an accumulation of tools and other goods that, taken together, facilitate further production.

With Mill came a broader view of the processes of production and distribution. Distribution, he believed, could be affected by changes in social conventions, government intervention, and legislation. He favoured broader taxation, such as inheritance taxes to equalize incomes, as well as a greater stewardship of the nation's natural resources since they were a benefit to all and hence a public good.

Taken together, the factors of production – land, labour, capital, and entrepreneurship – made up society's production function until the early part of the twentieth century when the role of technology and technological innovations began to be accepted as more and more important.

Writing in 1912, Joseph Schumpeter posited that growth is a function of an exogenous shock to the production function arising from new innovation-based investment opportunities recognized by a few very gifted individuals. He argued that after each round of innovation there is increased borrowing and production. The original entrepreneurs are inevitably followed by "copy-cats," and the system eventually experiences overproduction and, finally, recession. But the equilibrium that is reached is done so at an ever-higher level of output. The new level is at a higher level of material wealth per person and a higher level of per capita income. For Schumpeter, economic growth and the creation of wealth occurs as the consequence of discontinuous bursts of creative entrepreneurial activity. In his view, either the creation of monopolies or the act of government intervention would inhibit the creation of wealth and, through a complex chain of events, such meddling with entrepreneurial activity would lead to socialism.

From the 1920s through the Second World War, the roles of production, innovation, entrepreneurship, and research and development, together with science and technology, were all seen as increasingly important to the production process and the wealth of nations. Knowledge was seen as an important part of the production function. All of these were added to the original factors of production – land, labour, and capital.

Society has now come to recognize that knowledge itself is a factor of production. Knowledge can be in the mind of a worker, embodied in software, or in the working of the computer itself. Brought to the production process, it adds value.

The nature of capital is changing. Once it referred to money used for investment; later it identified the range of products, including machine tools (tools used to make new tools), that were used to make new products. More and more, capital included human capital: the level and breadth of knowledge held by the population in general and workers in particular. Increasingly today one hears about the rise of the knowledge worker – people who bring to the production process complex chunks of knowledge.

The production process is itself becoming knowledge intensive. The machines contain bits and pieces of intelligence – whether it is in computer-controlled production, just-in-time inventory management, or in the widespread use of networked companies where information is shared on a real-time basis.

It is clear that a new economy is being put in place – an economy that produces and consumes intangibles. From computer-automated design to virtual-reality amusement devices to satellite imaging of resources and pollution, there has been and continues to be an inexorable move to an economy that depends on information and communications technologies. This new economy is being constructed in a global context.

Whereas Adam Smith's wealth of nations depended on specialization and a division of labour within nations, the new wealth of nations depends on information, communication technology, and in-depth knowledge – on a global basis. Globalization, driven by access to real-time global computer and other communications networks, is being done by multinational and transnational institutions of all types. The global economy is characterized by a restless search for new products, new ideas, and new content. A model of the new economy is the entertainment industry. Based on software and images, today's product is soon eclipsed by another and another, with seemingly no end in sight.

As machine tools characterized the industrial age, software is the "machine tool" of the information age. The term software is used in the broadest sense, from instructing machines how to perform, to controlling satellites and telephone switches, to the creation of content for an advertising campaign or for a major motion picture. Where the old economy was one of things, of tangibles, the new economy is one of knowledge, images, and concepts – of intangibles.

The new wealth of nations has a capital base of knowledge and software. The new resource of the information age is information itself: in home, educational, entertainment, or industrial applications. The machine tool companies of the new economy are those that build things upon which yet more intangible things can be built. Some of the "machine tool companies" of the information age are Microsoft, WordPerfect, Borland, and Sony. Each of these companies is devoted to producing the intangible software that is more and more at the heart of new global and national wealth.

In the information age the production function has changed. Adam Smith talked about economies of scale; today we talk about flexibility and adaptability. To the traditional mix of land, labour, capital, and entrepreneurship is today added some mix of information/knowledge/technology.

Information and related communications technology is transforming society and the nature of work. A new resource has been created, one that, in turn, creates new wealth. But how are the benefits from the new wealth being distributed? The Mercantilists favoured one class, the Physiocrats another. Each approach resulted in disparities in both income and status. Are we now creating new class disparities with the introduction of the new technologies?

Before we turn to address this question in the next section, let us consider a related question: Are there hidden or social costs to information and communications technologies? We know some of the obvious costs and benefits, but what are some of the less obvious? Society embraced the automobile and found that this transformative technology turned society inside out. But balanced against its benefits should be weighed a host of social costs – including over 50,000 traffic deaths a year in North America alone.

There are powerful advantages inherent in ICT. What makes it a transformative technology is that it is labour-saving, energy saving, and capital saving. Thus, among other advantages, it is environmentally clean, productive, efficient, and relatively cheap; as well, it uses less labour and creates high-level jobs for software designers. The benefits of ICT are being heralded in the daily media and are especially "hyped" by those who can immediately appropriate those benefits in the "bottom line."

But there is a downside. As ICT rolls through the economy, it appears to be leading to, or at least contributing to, falling real incomes, deskilling, structural unemployment, deteriorating standards of living, and likely social and political instability. There are also other costs that come from living, working, and governing in a real-time world.

Mention should also be made of the ongoing concerns relating to ergonomics, radiation, and eyestrain. Some costs, such as radiation, may only be fully understood in a longer timeframe – after many have sustained injuries. Other costs are more diffuse and apply to larger groups in society, or to society itself. While it is difficult to make the case for caution since the costs are so widespread, we should nevertheless still be concerned: while the cost to each individual may be small, taken together the costs to all may be very great. In this way some of the social costs associated with ICT may be similar to the problems connected with the ozone layer; the costs are costs borne by everyone. It is therefore not clear who should take the lead in fixing things. "Everybody's problem is nobody's problem," is an old maxim that helps to understand why social costs are often so difficult to address.

Disparities in society

According to Nobel laureate Abdus Salam, some 900 years ago an Islamic physician divided his pharmacopoeia into "Diseases of the Rich and Diseases of the Poor." Today, he says, "Half the treatise would refer to the disease of the rich as fear of annihilation whereas that of the poor would be of hunger and starvation." It is a perceptive and powerful comment on the nature of the disparities that threaten the stability of the world today.

Disparity has taken on many meanings. It is used to describe situations where equitable access to reasonable working conditions and economic returns does not exist; where access to education and training is available only to the privileged; where access to a free press and public libraries is often restricted; where access to a healthy and peaceful environment seems hopeless, and where access to a variety of political beliefs is difficult, if not impossible. Its most common use, however, is still to describe the economic differences between the rich and the poor.

The contrast between life in suburbia and that in the inner cities of the United States is almost beyond comprehension. If the American dream still exists, it must be a nightmare for those who live without hope of employment in the new ghettos. But that difference dwarfs the comparison between life in the industrialized world and what is happening to those five billion or so persons who inhabit the remaining regions.

Although some in the Middle and Far East appear to be making progress, the numbers are still startling. The fact that the gross domestic product per capita of the Group of Seven industrial nations in 1988 was shown as US$23,000 whereas in the same year the *World Development Report* from the World Bank[4] placed the more than 40 very poor countries at under US$450 provides a dramatic contrast. According to former West German chancellor Willy Brandt,[5] in this century in the developing countries 250 million people have fled their homes, 15 million children have died each year before their fifth birthday and 300 million children have not gone to school at all (and these numbers do not take into account the recent and ongoing carnage in Rwanda and Zaire). In the U.S. there is one doctor for 520 people; in Ethiopia there is one for 58,000. Given these contrasts, we are talking about disparity in much more than financial terms.

No matter how we define "well off," there is a huge gap between those who are and those who are not. It is not only between nations that the gap exists; it pervades every corner of our society. In the United States the poverty rate for blacks (34 per cent) is three times that for whites. More than 60 per cent of women in the world suffer from poverty and sexual discrimination, and thousands of homeless in the "developed world" spend nights in doorways, alleys, and underground bypasses. From 1979 to 1986 federal spending (U.S.) on natural resources was cut by 24 per cent, on non-military research by 24 per cent, on aid to schools by 14 per cent and on energy preparedness by 65 per cent. Among families in Canada the rate of poverty has been on the increase since 1981. In the 1960s there were primarily four groups: the elderly, the disabled, native peoples, and those living in depressed areas. Today there are three: women, natives, and the disabled, with the unemployed young an emerging fourth.[6]

The disparity in income and in quality of life between the haves and the have-nots has been put forward from time to time as the principal cause of both the French and Russian Revolutions, the Great Depression of the 1930s, and the rise of Communism. This premise was based on the lack of what we now refer to as the middle class. In an article in the *Atlantic Monthly* (May 1994), Jack Beatty postulated that it was an expanding middle class that got in the way of the realization of the Marxist prediction that capitalism would inevitably collapse.

If it is true that the middle class has been the buffer between political stability and revolution, then that buffer is beginning to erode with alarming speed. According to Beatty, after 1973 the median family income (adjusted for inflation) in the U.S. began to decrease, despite the fact that the number of two-income families was increasing. Census figures indicate that since 1980 the number of households deemed to be middle class fell from 71 to 63 per cent, while those in the low-income bracket went up by more than a third. The number of white-collar managers and executives experienced a reduction of 0.8 per cent, technical workers, 2.9 per cent, and those with college education, 2.5 per cent. Hardest hit were workers with a high school education or less. The former experienced a drop of 14.7 per cent while the latter a staggering 21.7 per cent. Lester Thurow is quoted as saying, "Earning prospects are collapsing for the bottom two-thirds of the workforce."

Not so, reports Beatty, for those at the top. In the last decade, the number of Americans earning more than $500,000 a year increased by 985 per cent and the combined salaries of those making more than $1,000,000 went up by 2,184 per cent. In April 1996, a special report on executive pay by the *Wall Street Journal* noted: "The earnings gap between executives at the very top of corporate America and middle managers and workers has stretched into a vast chasm." In 1995 the CEOs of major companies received compensation 212 times higher than the average worker. That's a five-fold increase from 1965, when the multiple was 44.[7]

Jim Dator, one of the founders of the World's Future Studies Federation, put it this way: "One per cent of the families in the United States own over 40 per cent of the nation's net worth and 50 per cent of the net financial assets." Disparity in the distribution of skills and wealth has always been with us, but never more so than in the age of information and communications technology.

Ironically, the new wealth created by ICT seems to be bringing with it many of the new disparities that Beatty and others report, namely: the declining middle class, poverty amidst plenty, and the substitution of bi-modal distribution for the traditional income curve, which underlines the common perception that the rich are getting richer and the poor, poorer. Added to this is the growing gap between the wages and opportunities available to the skilled and the unskilled, between those who understand or can operate the technology and those who feel bewildered and left behind.

As pointed out in a previous publication,[8] added to the skill/income problem is a parallel rise in nonstandard employment such as part-time work, short-term work, and self-employment. Most part-time workers are classed as "involuntary" part-time; that is, they would prefer regular jobs. In Canada, nonstandard jobs account for nearly half of all new jobs and now represent nearly 30 per cent of total employment.

With information technology, certain kinds of work can be done anywhere and purchased as needed. The finished work is delivered via fax or telecom lines from computers. The "anytime, anyplace" workforce is one that is distributed – often working from home. This can leave the worker in a weakened position.

Unable to collaborate with fellow workers, these "independent" teleworkers are often without negotiating power. Without any bargaining strength they make up a new electronic cottage industry. Since the influence of labour unions is minimized, labour becomes a variable rather than a fixed cost. This means that overhead costs are kept down and the labour, when acquired, is cheaper, since there are few, if any, employee benefits to be paid out.

Despite the increased productivity and many benefits that accrue from the introduction of the new technological tools, society is going through a particularly difficult period. Not too long ago, a single-wage earner could support a spouse, clothe, feed, and educate two or more children, and buy a new car and home. Today we have moved to a situation where two-wage families seem to be the norm and, often, even a dual-income household is not enough to maintain what was formerly considered a middle-class existence. We seem to be moving to a two-tier society where the poor, including the working poor, and the rich will see each other across a great unbridgeable divide.

The situation has been compared to that of a Boeing 747 aircraft, where at one end of the multimillion dollar machine are the highly skilled pilot, co-pilot, and navigator and at the other end, in the cabin, are the flight attendants. One does not become a pilot by working for the same airline as a flight attendant. Rather, it is necessary to drop out and be retrained for the more skilled and highly paid job. The skills profile of our society will tend more and more to resemble this analogy. One group of people will push buttons, monitor lights, and make simple repairs. Another group will design the hardware and software which make the system function. In between there will be a declining demand for the semi-skilled worker. Broadening the 747 analogy: What about the passengers who are transported, fed, and amused? Is this the likely outcome for the great mass of our population, who are no longer able to find satisfying work or any kind of work at all? Will we have to provide entertainment, food, alcohol, and drugs to the unemployed mass of the population to keep them amused through the journey of life?

The implications of disparity are far reaching. In communications the receiver is essential to the transmitter. It is equally true that every seller needs a buyer. With almost four-fifths of the world in poverty, it is difficult to see how a global economy can function. As the number of poor increases within nations, the costs of social services together with national, corporate, and consumer debt rise. Purchasing power declines, followed by reduced profits and opportunities for entrepreneurs in the free market of the future. Even from the point of view of "enlightened self-interest," owners and managers of capital everywhere should view growing disparity as a threat.

Habitually prevalent unemployment has also led to the creation of a welfare class. The seeming inability of leaders to provide suitable jobs for those unable to find work, combined with the rising cost of "safety nets," has resulted in a lack of confidence in elected political leaders and a growing cynicism regarding the political-economic system itself. With a two-tier society characterized by more and more disparity, there is a corresponding increase in social unrest and crime. The feeling becomes, "If I can't get what I need or want one way, then I'll get it another."

For the past many years, status in society has been determined, in part, by earnings and position. Doctors and other professionals used to rank highest in status, with manual labour – including some sales jobs – ranking lowest. When strangers meet at a party or conference, a common ground for discussion is often how they describe themselves in terms of what they do for a living. If the lower tier in society, including the working poor, those without jobs, and the diminished middle class, no longer take pride in their place in society – if work has lost its savour – then the effect on the perceived quality of life will surely be negative.

In the "old days" people didn't focus so directly on quality of life. People grew up: they were educated, got jobs and careers, were married, and "settled down." The quality of their lives was a summation of the various choices and actions they took. Today we see quality of life as something that can be understood and managed in a rather self-conscious way by individuals and governments. An understanding of the elements that contribute to the quality of life is fundamental if we are to find solutions to the problems that have arisen as a result of the introduction of radically new electronic technologies.

Human needs and wants

What do we mean by "quality of life" and how does the nature of work fit into the description? Thomas Carlyle, in a rectorial address, called work the grand cure of all maladies that ever beset mankind. If he was right then we need that cure, for there certainly seem to be enough maladies today to satisfy the most pessimistic of observers. As one writer put it in commenting on the public mood during the 1994 mid-term U.S. elections, "Americans are angry... they are going through 'tough times' and don't see the benefits of an economy that is supposed to be growing. Real wages have declined 9.6 per cent from 1979 to 1993. Jobs are less secure, companies are contracting-out rather than hiring full-time employees and adult children without jobs are moving back home."[9] As Stendhal pointed out, "Without work the vessel of life has no ballast." And there seems to be a lack of ballast, or at least a lack of the right kind of ballast, in this age of information.

Quality of life is an expression that has been used in many contexts, contexts that change with the prevailing culture, religion, and contemporary value systems. One writer described it this way: "The quality of life of a group or nation depends on the dynamics of the needs, on the satisfaction or non-satisfaction of those needs, and on social character. And just like lifestyle, that quality of life also has as many components as there are needs."[10] This is true, but two considerations seem to dominate the thinking today: one is global and the other more personal and local.

The Interaction Council, a think tank of twenty political leaders chaired by Maria de Lourds Pintasilago, the former prime minister of Portugal, is concerned with the global aspect. Its deliberations and reports relate to such matters as: the fight against absolute poverty; disparity between the four-fifths of the world's population who must make do with 20 per cent of the world's natural resources compared with the other fifth's 80 per cent; the plight of women; population growth; increasing social and environmental damage; and the growth in military spending despite the end of the Cold War (US$815 billion in 1992).

These are critical issues that deserve the attention of such an august group, but they do not deal with the concerns of the new unemployed, the poor, and the declining middle class referred to in the previous section. At the personal and local level many individuals, perhaps the majority, included in that fortunate upper one-fifth of the population referred to by the Council, are themselves troubled and becoming increasingly fearful about the kind of world they are leaving to their children and grandchildren. Their fear has much to do with the rapidity of the changes that are taking place in the workplace.

Newspaper accounts note that the middle class feels threatened. It is threatened. "Feelings of economic uncertainty, once the prerogative of manual workers, have now bitten deep into white-collar middle classes.... almost all professional people, managers and office staff no longer feel safe." (Anthony King, *Daily Telegraph*, January 1995.) "The great western middle class is feeling sick. It is witnessing its own demise: the collapse of socialism has coincided with the advance of a new proletariat, the short-term contract technological consultant. Today, the dominant reality is that of an unpredictable, post-industrial world." (James Morgan, *Financial Times*, January 1995).

It is true that global and local interests overlap in places. The growth in military spending, the status of women, and the environment are cases in point. And things are being done at the local level. Opportunities for women in the workplace are increasing. Many communities are becoming more and more concerned with environmental issues. For example, the use of recycling systems is increasing, and groups are found protesting against various threats to forests, lakes, endangered species, and so on. At the same time, as insolvent governments cut back on social safety nets, the growth of poverty at home is more and more becoming a topic attractive to columnists and other writers on the pages of some periodicals and newspapers. But these concerns seem to pale by comparison with the struggle of individuals to survive the demoralizing fluctuations in their economic and social status occasioned by the information and technological revolutions. The magnitude and the speed of the changes predicted in 1970 in Alvin Toffler's *Future Shock* seem overwhelming to young and old alike.

What is it that people want? On the surface it appears to be more and more consumer goods. In Neil Postman's book *Amusing Ourselves to Death*, the author charges that television is becoming increasingly trivial and shallow. Although this is true of television, it is also typical of what is happening in Western society as a whole. The shelves and floors of department stores are filled with virtually every possible gadget imaginable but, as one investigator said, "despite the two-fold increase in per capita spending for personal consumption the number of Americans describing themselves as very happy is no larger than it was in 1957."[11] The notion that more of everything will produce happiness is turning out to be a chimera.

Abraham Maslow held that there is a hierarchy of needs. Once basic physical needs such as food, clothing, and shelter are satisfied, he believed that they are superseded by a dominating need for safety, love, power, self-actualization, and aesthetic appreciation.[12] Some years earlier, Joseph McCulley, the progressive headmaster of Pickering College in Canada, had put forward his own list, which included the need for success, affection, and recognition.

One of the most comprehensive analyses of basic human needs was put forward in 1977 by John and Magda Cordell McHale.[13] As stated in the preface of the report, their purpose was to provide quantitative assessments of human needs as to food, health, shelter, and clothing, and to consider how these might be reasonably met, given the cultural and individual differences that exist in such a far-reaching investigation.

In the Introduction to the McHales' study, Harlan Cleveland referred to the United Nations' 1948 *Universal Declaration of Human Rights* and quoted the following sections:

> Article 22: Everyone, as a member of society, has the right to social security and is entitled to realization, through

national effort and international cooperation and in accordance with the organization and resources of each state, of the economic, social and cultural rights indispensable for his dignity and the free development of his personality.

Article 25: 1. Everyone has the right to a standard of living adequate for the health and wellbeing of himself and of his family, including food, clothing, housing and medical care and necessary social services, and the right to security in the event of unemployment, sickness, disability, widowhood, old age or other lack of livelihood in circumstances beyond his control.

Article 26: 1. Everyone has the right to education. Education shall be free, at least in the elementary and fundamental stages. Elementary education shall be compulsory. Technical and professional education shall be made generally available and higher education shall be equally accessible to all on the basis of merit.

The Declaration was a very effective way of codifying many of the essential elements of a civil society, and Cleveland was moved to say, "Basic human needs have 'arrived'." And, in a sense, they seemed to have done just that. The early 1970s was marked by increased awareness of the relationship between needs, wants, and the human predicament.

Along with the "rights" articulated in the UN declaration came increased recognition of the need to conserve nonrenewable resources. Schumacher had written Small Is Beautiful and The Ecologist had come out with Blueprint for Survival, an ideological prototype for "green party" movements in Europe. The most dramatic impact, however, was made by the Club of Rome, when it published Limits to Growth, a report that garnered world-wide interest in the fragile environment and the complexity of the interrelationships that affect not only the environment but other world problems as well. The book sold literally millions of copies and became the inspiration for a series of national associations associated with the Club. New organizations seemed to be sprouting everywhere, not just concerned with environmental issues and human needs, but also devoted to improving the lot of the disadvantaged and other individuals handicapped in one way or another.

However all was far from sweetness and light, especially when viewed from a geo-political perspective. The United States was mired in a devastating war in Vietnam, which not only pitted the world's most powerful military machine against a small opponent but also created divisions within families and neighbours at home that have carried over to this day. The same country which, just a few decades earlier, had conceived and successfully executed the visionary and humanitarian "Marshall Plan" to help rebuild a shattered Europe – enemies and friends alike – now was earning the soubriquet "the ugly Americans." Obviously this was not what Americans needed or wanted.

After Vietnam and the Watergate scandal, which brought down President Nixon's administration in the United States, the brief period of international idealism that had characterized the post-Second World War period seemed to have come to an end. Even the collapse of Communism in Eastern Europe, which one writer was moved to hail as "the end of history," failed to herald a new era of confidence among the industrialized nations of the West. Although attempts have been underway to achieve a political union in Europe, the going has been far from easy. Problems have been exacerbated by an economic recession accompanied by rising national deficits as governments strive to maintain existing services. The only response to gain credence in the popular media has been a negative one: that is, reduce government spending even in such formerly sacrosanct areas as health and education. As one columnist in *The Globe and Mail* wrote, "...the point is no one's really looking for solutions anyway."[14]

While it is our belief that freedom, identity and security, together with the material requirements for survival, are the common factors that appear on virtually every list of human needs, our concern is not to produce a study on needs and wants, but to make the point that enlightened self-interest and Lincoln's "Government of, for and by the people" require that the new wealth of nations be shared equitably so that the needs and desires of the peoples of the world can be addressed, and that this ought not to be accomplished through handouts, but by taking advantage of the economic strengths inherent in information technology to provide work that is socially useful and individually satisfying.

It may seem to be a truism, as Adam Smith said, that "Consumption is the sole end and purpose of all production; and the interest of the producer ought to be attended to only so far as it is necessary for promoting that of the consumer." But, as the author of the article cited in the opening section was quick to point out, "the logic held up only so long as the individual remained both the consuming and producing unit. But in the modern world, the great majority of production is done not by individuals but by complex organizations. In this kind of system, the simplicity of automatic exchange between individual and consumers ... almost disappears."[15] It is these labyrinth-like organizations, in a time when electronic networks are world-wide, that hold the real power rather than the nation-states. Given this situation, the future of democracy may be at stake unless steps are taken at an international level to find appropriate methods of taxing the multinational corporations in order to return power to elected governments, who, in turn, can develop the policies which will ensure that the needs of their citizens are met.

The developments described above lead us to a discussion of the global marketplace and how the introduction of the new technologies, although undoubtedly creating new wealth, has, at the same time, made it more difficult for jurisdictions to meet the legitimate needs of, and provide a reasonable quality of life for, their citizens.

Globalization

The technologies of transportation and communication have always played a role in economic growth, whether of regions, or nations, or even the entire globe.

From covered wagons to sailing ships, developing transportation technologies opened up markets and developed the economies of nations by expanding trade and commerce. Often one nation benefited at the expense of others, taking over entirely, in the quest for markets and power, the affairs of another nation. The British Empire, for example, used the technologies of transportation to its own ends. The East India Company and the Hudson's Bay Company are cases in point.

These early examples of world trade were tied to the transportation and communication systems of the day. Sailing and steamships permitted one kind of development; computer networks and satellite communications permit another.

It can be argued that the technological developments from 1600 to 1900 favoured growing integration within and among nations. The development of the railway is a good example. This technology was a prime instrument of nation-building. So important was the railway to Canada's development that it was referred to as the "national dream." The technologies of the sailing ship and steam engine tended to strengthen domestic economies and broaden the international reach of nations.

Another technology of nation-building was the creation of a system of canals in Europe and North America. Beginning as far back as the sixteenth century in Europe and continuing to the Erie Canal system in the United States, new ways of transporting goods led to a broadening of commerce. Canals also led to a strengthening of international ties: the Suez Canal and the Panama Canal are notable examples. Just as ties were strengthened by the growing commerce between nations, the technologies of transportation and communication at the same time tended to strengthen the integrity of individual nations.

The development of commercial instruments such as stocks and bonds, and the creation of markets or exchanges where they could be bought and sold, also spurred trade between nations. In the 1800s investment between nations had been primarily in the form of bonds and other forms of loans. Major markets in places such as London and New York would lend money in the form of bonds to foreign governments. The foreign governments would use the money for infrastructure development of one type or another; chiefly railroads, highways, and electric power developments. Later, investment was more and more by direct ownership, or equity. Here a corporation would directly invest in another country either by creating a subsidiary or by buying 51 percent ownership in an existing foreign enterprise. This launched the era of the multinational corporation. Before the Second World War the multinational firms were few in number and were primarily headquartered in Europe. During the 1950s, 1960s, and 1970s, the U.S. firms went multinational. They extended their operations to all areas of the world where they were allowed to do business. Today multinationals have headquarters in many countries and do business just about everywhere.

Globalization rests on an infrastructure of inexpensive, reliable, and accessible instantaneous communications. First it was the telegraph, then the telephone and fax. Today, the key innovation has been the conversion of information, whether as sound, pictures, text, or numbers, into streams of digitized "bits." Digitization means that information can be manipulated at high speed by computers. The exponential increase in computing power over the past 20 years, coupled with dramatic reductions in cost, have made computer applications more affordable in all parts of our economy. At the same time, the development of inexpensive fibre optic cable, new wireless technologies, satellites, digital compression, and switching techniques allow these digital bit-streams to be communicated at high speed over a wide variety of wireless and telephone national and global networks. It is now possible to exchange information anywhere in any format, and to conduct transactions electronically over any distance.[16]

The growing transactions that define globalization tend to draw the nations of the world ever closer while diminishing the importance and potential role of the nation-state. International agreements such as the European Union, the North American Free Trade Agreement, and international trade agreements such as the General Agreement on Tariffs and Trade, as well as the growth of non-governmental organizations, all seem to be eclipsing the role of the nation. Outside the political arena, the internationalization of corporations and their many transactions between headquarters and subsidiaries also help to foster this globalization.

The individual economic actors seem to be moving from the

national stages of various countries to the international stage. As they interact with each other directly in real time, using a variety of communications networks, the role of the nation-state becomes somewhat blurred. Also blurred is the extent to which the nation-state can exert power, influence, and control over its economy and domestic marketplace. National economies seem to be taking second place as the multinational companies, money traders, and dealers in monetary assets of all types around the world seek the best returns, the highest yields. To put it bluntly, as globalization grows, the power and sovereignty of individual nations is circumscribed. While some may applaud the weakening of the nation-state, there are consequences for individual citizens.

With globalization, domestic labour in the developed world increasingly finds itself competing with labour from low-wage areas. Often low-wage areas are low in other areas as well: they often have little or no environmental protection, few health-care or pension benefits, and nonexistent or unenforced child labour laws. Low-wage areas are often kept low because labour is not allowed to organize to bargain collectively for better wages and benefits.

With globalization the developed world finds itself competing with the formerly separate markets of Asia and Latin America. Jobs in factories from all sectors of the economy have moved offshore. Firms using information technologies can issue orders, manage inventories, buy resources, design products, or do research just about anywhere in the world. Firms can bring together all factors of production to produce goods and services anywhere on earth: global information and communication technologies mean that corporations can have a virtual presence anywhere. With global brand names, the final product is produced anywhere; the final product is sold anywhere.

Global networks mean that work can be done elsewhere and imported into a developed nation by satellite or ground links. New computer-related jobs have emerged in Barbados, the Philippines, and Ireland. Software is written overseas where skills can often be obtained at one-fifth to one-third of the cost in North America. For example, Bangalore, in India, is emerging as a centre of software expertise. There is a growing global competition for the "good jobs" that are to be found in the "new economy."

Ireland is pursuing an information-age development strategy using broadband systems and "state-of-the-art" telecommunications systems so that workers can remain in Ireland and yet be part of a U.S. firm. One California firm uses a 1-800 number so that clients can get immediate help from its software engineers. As the day wears on, calls are handed over to the firm's Irish office. Here high value-added workers take the call and help the client resolve the problem. The client is unaware and, most likely, indifferent as to where the help came from. The company benefits, since it finds that its Irish workers cost less, work harder, and have less turnover.

Information technology is distance and time insensitive. Globalization implies the increasing porosity of national boundaries. The notion of a Canadian workforce doing 9 to 5 activities in a jurisdiction called Canada is rapidly eroding. We have gone through the competition with low-wage countries in textiles, electronics, and other manufactured products. Now a sophisticated information infrastructure promises to make service workers halfway around the world competitive with Canadians. Software, telephone order takers, data entry, on-line data bases, et cetera, can be located wherever the skills exist at the lowest cost. What are the long-term implications for developed countries such as Canada? What about the mix of skills needed? Maintaining a high standard of living means providing high value-added jobs in Canada: how will this be accomplished in the context of globalization?

Going global is the phenomenon where activities going on somewhere in the world are relevant for someone somewhere else: the interested parties include multinational firms, banks, governments, and citizens. Everybody and everything is connected in a delicate interconnected networked globe. Ultimately all citizens of the world become linked in a complex web held together by communications networks. Response is, more and more, needed and expected in real time. We are moving to a 24-hour workday.

Questions of time management and personal stress arise as the workday blurs and as the value and rate of global trading rises. Stock market closings in New York are followed by closings in Vancouver, Tokyo, Hong Kong, London, and New York again. Foreign exchange trading has soared. *The Economist* magazine rates it at 1.3 trillion dollars per day! Cross-border transactions in bonds and equities have surged from 3 percent of United States GDP in 1970 to 136 percent in 1995.[17] The race may go not to the nimble but to those who can operate with very little sleep or who can manage their time, and stress levels, most effectively.

The stress associated with a global 24-hour day goes beyond the banks, stock markets, and multinationals. It is increasingly common to watch morning television and see an interview with someone in another time zone and learn of a market collapse, or a bombing, or a kidnapping. With the strong visuals of global satellite television, we are suddenly jolted awake and learn that something has happened during the night that will have an affect on us during our workday. What are the implications for a nation and its citizens, as workers. What are the implications for government?

While most can recall the mantra of "thinking globally but acting locally," a question arises as to the role of nation-states. It may be that globalization is leading to a reversal of the mantra; it may be that the new reality is one where acting globally and thinking locally is all that nation-states can effectively manage. Acting globally will not be easy since it will demand collaboration and consensus on a scale and to a degree that is normally associated with emergencies of one sort or another: a time when the nation-state is itself threatened.

Consider, too, the challenge to community posed by the growing proliferation of computer networks. More and more people are communicating with others on the basis of shared concerns. We are seeing discussions carried out on networks about a wide range of issues with others from around the world. With the dramatic rise of the Internet, people are getting to "know" the abstract entities they communicate with over computer networks better than they know their next-door neighbours. The concept of community is radically challenged and is in the process of being redefined. We are seeing a movement away from geographical communities to concern- or interest-driven communities where the participants can be across town, in another country, or around the world.

The relative newness of globalization has caught governments off guard. It was thought that governments could issue a policy here, monitor a development there, and in general, muddle through. But global networks are transformative. Globalization challenges the authority of existing institutions.

The role of the nation-state is being reviewed. With porous borders and blurring boundaries, governments in the developed areas have to grapple with a host of issues that don't lend themselves to easy solutions: the economic and political power of the multinationals; capital "flightiness" to tax havens; harmonization among all countries leading to possible lowered wages and environmental controls; the opening up of the domestic labour force to global competition.

The new wealth of nations means that governments have to develop policies for the following propositions: that information has emerged as a strategic resource that leads to new ways of organizing and achieving consensus; that economic independence has given way to economic interdependence; that having a work force that knows how to use computers is just as important as having an economy that produces computers; and that the range of information technologies that make up the information infrastructure of an economy can yield a competitive advantage in a complex, global, interdependent world where decisions and responses are taking place in "real time."

A borderless world has emerged. Satellite communications and real-time transactions have linked the global business centres. Services flow between countries. The technology is distance insensitive. When economies were based on "land, labour, and capital," barriers could be set up to control the movement of goods, people, and money, so as to protect and advance national interests. This is impossible when everything is increasingly based on flows of electronic information through global networks. How can a nation promote the wealth and welfare of its citizens in the information age? What are "national interests" in an increasingly globalized world?

National government intervention of the past may no longer be possible or desirable in the borderless, global world of tomorrow. National jurisdictions may prove difficult or impossible to regulate; perhaps regulation can only be achieved at a different level: more local in some instances and more global in others.

Consider the emergence of global standards. Harmonization is taking place in many areas. Converging standards will affect the regulatory regimes of all countries. Ways of doing things that have gone on without question will be challenged by cheaper and faster methods of "doing business." Regulations concerning stock transactions and banking, environmental controls, occupational health and safety, etc., will be challenged as harmonization begins to take place. How will any nation cope? How will harmonization take place?

Nations are finding it increasingly difficult to manage their national economies. Globalization means that monetary and fiscal policies are tied to developments elsewhere. Few nations are so powerful that they can follow an independent monetary or fiscal policy. Most are tied to international market developments. Fearful of changes to the value of their currencies or to the prospect of an international bond market that reevaluates their risk, most national governments have little room for new policies.

While globalization is taking place, while the "wheeling and dealing" goes on 24 hours a day, every day, the citizens of nation-states still need to rely on their local nation-states. While the economy seems to have gone global, the nation-state is the place where citizens turn for a host of services: from education to medical care to income support when jobs are lost. The nation-state provides the social and physical infrastructure in which individuals come into the world, are educated, raise families, find meaningful work, and finally leave the world.

Although the role of the nation-state is undergoing a reevaluation, there are bills to be paid! Unemployed workers need support, the health-care establishment has to be maintained and upgraded, the educational sector is constantly asked to produce brighter and better graduates, and a physical infrastructure of public goods such as roads, bridges, sewers, and airports needs to maintained and upgraded.

How does the nation meet the fiscal challenge in a globalized economy? How does the nation find the tax base in a porous globalized world to provide for its citizens? How do the developed countries of today avoid becoming part of the Third World of tomorrow's information-based global economy?

We turn now to the question of taxes and consider how it may be possible to find a new tax base, one that is at the heart of globalization, but one that is accessible by nations; a tax that is appropriate to a new economy; a tax that offers a way to get at the productivity of the new economy, and become a source of income to ensure national fiscal soundness.

Taxes

In 1789 Benjamin Franklin, in a letter referring to the long-term prospects for the U. S. Constitution, wrote that there is very little about which one can be certain in life: "...everything appears to promise that (the Constitution) will last; but in this world nothing is certain but death and taxes." And in 1904, U.S. Supreme Court Justice Oliver Wendell Holmes, Jr. wrote in a decision that "Taxes are what we pay for civilized society."

Taxes have always been with us. Taxes on consumption were levied in ancient Greece and in Rome. Taking the form of import tariffs, these were a means of raising funds. Net worth taxes, including property taxes, also date from the earliest times. In the time of Julius Caesar, a 1 per cent general sales tax was introduced. Head taxes and other taxes were introduced, some having to do with agricultural production. The Middle Ages saw changes that included the rise of indirect taxes such as transit duties and market access fees, plus taxes on certain foods and beverages. In addition there was a spread of land and property taxes.

Taxation is a legal way for governments to gain money or other valuables from individuals and organizations. Taxes can be collected in the form of money or commodities. Depending on the soundness of the money, payment can be made in kind. In

American frontier settlements of the eighteenth and early nineteenth centuries, local governments commonly imposed taxes by requiring that each adult male work a given number of days constructing community facilities such as roads and schools.

This example points to the most commonly cited need for taxation: to provide for communities those goods or services that everybody wants, but that will not be provided in adequate quantities by the market system alone. In addition to private goods, communities need public goods. The government needs tax dollars to build schools, roads, sewers, and lighthouses, or to maintain a standing army. Some of the productive potential of the economy is redirected from private ends to public ends. The changing shape of production has an impact on the type and way in which taxes are collected. The more productive the economy, the wealthier the nation, the greater can be the amount of taxes collected.

Taxes are also generally deemed acceptable for fiscal or budgetary reasons; to manage macroeconomic policy goals such as full employment, economic growth, etc.; or for social or redistributive reasons, to lessen inequalities in the distribution of income.

A typical tax has at least three elements: a definition of the group or item to be taxed (the base), the rate structure, and an identification of the taxpayer. The base or item taxed tends to change over time. With new activities come new taxes: early taxes on property have been overtaken by taxes on motor vehicles, gasoline taxes, and other forms of taxes relating to the automobile. New forms of production lead to new regimes for tax collection.

A widely used distinction is between "direct" and "indirect" taxes. A direct tax is one which the legal taxpayer pays directly – examples are income and property taxes. Indirect taxes are paid as part of buying something else: an excise tax on liquor or cigarettes or a value-added tax. With indirect taxes, the collector of the taxes (e.g., the cigarette seller) usually acts for the government with the final tax paid by the purchaser of the product. An overall rule of thumb is that direct taxes tend to be more progressive, while indirect taxes tend to be regressive.

A progressive tax is one that increases more in relation to income than would a strictly proportional tax that takes a fixed percentage of income from each person. A regressive tax takes a larger fraction from a low-income earner than a high-income earner. Fixed taxes are regressive, since the fixed amount to be paid is trivial to a rich person but can be damaging to the poor person. The income tax system is progressive; with increased earnings, the individual moves to a higher marginal tax bracket. Incremental earnings are taxed at a higher rate. Progressive tax systems are deemed more equitable from the principle of ability to pay. With greater discretionary income, the wealthy are held to be better able to pay the progressively higher tax.

A theoretical discussion of taxes generally includes the question of tax burden. That is, in any given tax, who actually bears the burden of the tax? For example, an excise tax on alcohol, or any indirect tax, for that matter, is usually collected by one party (the manufacturer) to be turned over to the government. Here the tax burden or incidence of taxation is on one party (the buyer or consumer of the alcohol) versus another (the manufacturer).

Taxes on products that are highly substitutable (or highly elastic in the jargon of economics) can lead to drastic drops in sales of the product, and to unemployment for those who used to produce the product. For example, a tax on one brand of chocolate bar would likely lead to a mass switch to a competing brand. Here the incidence would fall on the maker of the chocolate bar, the workers, and those who supplied the raw materials. Governments usually try to impose indirect taxes on products that can't readily be substituted (which in economic jargon are said to be price inelastic).

Personal income taxes generally fall on the individual. These taxes are hard to shift. Corporate taxes can be borne by the corporation or, depending on market conditions, can be passed along to the final buyer in the form of a price increase. If profits are high in a particular industry and if the tax is small in relation to earnings, and if the corporation is concerned that an increase in price may lead to a fall off in sales, then the incidence of the tax will be borne by the corporations in any given industrial sector.

The history of taxation is a reflection of the state of the economy. In the earliest days, as noted, the tax was often a payment in kind. People were asked to donate labour or materials of some sort. With a functioning money system, taxes were levied on commodities – usually those with an inelastic demand. Thus the state would levy taxes on those products where, when prices were increased by the amount of the tax, sales would remain constant or would drop off only very slightly.

Today we see a transition to a new economy, one characterized by the production, storage, manipulation, and distribution of information. There is a growing tendency to see information, in all it forms, as the new natural resource of the economy. Many articles, books, and other publications mention the manifold ways in which information has augmented productivity. But there are huge costs involved in building an information economy. There are infrastructure costs and there are human costs as well.

The much talked about information highway is a growing reality. An interactive system to all homes and offices capable of carrying voice, text, and video is an eventual certainty. It will be built by new or existing enterprises. More than likely most, but not all, costs will be borne by the builders of the system. Payment will come from consumers, but support for the myriad functions that government must perform will also be needed. Ensuring that standards are developed, privacy protected, and security ensured is but a small part of the eventual role of government.

But there are broader considerations. The transition to a new economy means that we are moving from an economy that is producing and consuming tangibles, or things, to one that is producing and consuming intangibles – information in all its forms.

The intangible information of the new economy can be an utterance, an email message, a fax to one part of the globe or another, or a video delivered on-demand over cable. While value is created with each new information transaction, the new value or product travelling in a digital bit-stream over telecom, satellite, or cable is usually invisible, ephemeral – most often untaxable.

As networks become more secure, people are buying more and more things through them. Purchases paid for by credit cards or the new forms of electronic or computer-based cash, known as digital cash, are fast becoming a reality. The Internet is experiencing a surge in electronic commerce: stock trading, buying books, music, or digitized photographs and illustrations, computer software, electronic auctions, gambling, real estate sales, and more. These activities are taking place now, with more being planned. Much more.

Digital networks are distance insensitive. Data can be stored, manipulated, sent, and sold virtually anywhere. Payment can come from anywhere on the planet. With no cash, no receipts, and no papertrail, it is quite a job for the tax collector! How will local and national taxes be collected, who will collect them, and on whose behalf?

Currently, most net-based merchants are following local jurisdiction rules on mail-order purchases. As the *Wall Street Journal* noted on 21 November 1996, what difference does it make whether the order came from the Web or through a toll-free number?

But what happens when music isn't shipped on CDs, but is sent as a digital bit-stream downloaded from the Internet instead? When that happens, is it still a CD for tax purposes, or is it something else: an information service, perhaps subject to a different kind of tax, or to no tax at all? (In a digital world, how are the creators compensated for their work? What is the future of copyright?) What happens when other products and services are bought over the Net?

Note that the design of the Internet makes it impossible to determine with any certainty where someone making an electronic purchase is located. With typical mail-order, the product is shipped somewhere. But if the information is downloaded on the Internet, the seller may have no idea of its destination. And where does that seller reside? Where they actually sit? Where the server is? And consider what happens when payment is not made on a Visa or Mastercard, but rather by digital cash: an anonymous payment from one person to another with no third party intervention. Here the underground economy will truly have "gone digital."

With computer software, music, books, magazines, and business services all potentially headed for electronic distribution, governments will find themselves with very porous borders.

In the move to an economy of intangibles, it becomes nearly impossible to measure the transactions to be taxed since they occur on networks as a series of electronic impulses: a stream of digital information with trillions of ones and zeroes. The Information Society Project of the European Commission asks the question, "How will governments be able to continue to raise funds in an increasingly information-based world in which value is generated through systems and global networks, rather than through clearly identifiable material production and exchange?" With global electronic commerce expected to reach over $600 billion by the year 2000, this is a pressing question. One that becomes more urgent each day.

With information being encrypted in order to protect the security of the buyers, the possibility of tax evasion becomes much more likely. The same technology used to protect the buyers and sellers can also be used to keep the transaction itself a secret from tax authorities. As more commerce takes place on digital networks, it will be necessary for governments to develop fiscal tools that can work in the digital environment.

Another consequence as we change to an information economy is that much of the work formerly done by people is now done by computers: this is especially true for banks, offices, supermarkets, factories, and gas stations. Whether it is a customer using an ATM or pumping gas at a self-serve station, the ubiquitous availability of small, cheap microprocessors has meant the elimination of many, many jobs. Much of the intelligence displayed by humans in their work – the intelligence that went into remembering, deciding, ordering, guiding, or choosing – has now been incorporated into computer hardware and software.

As noted in a previous publication,[18] there is a growing number of people who are unemployed or are working part time at low-end "McJobs." These are people who used to work in "good" jobs in the industrial economy. From building ships, cars, steel, or television sets, they now find themselves displaced by computers or by the forces of globalization that dictate that products be built in the low-cost areas, that nations must be competitive even if it means that unemployment rolls rise throughout the developed world.

As a once-prosperous workforce is found to be redundant, two important things happen: first, people who once paid taxes are now without work and no longer pay taxes; second, these unemployed people now make demands on governments at all levels: for unemployment insurance, for retraining, for welfare.

Where will the new tax base be found? If the transition to an information economy goes on longer than most politicians are willing to admit, i.e., if the displaced workers never really find "good" jobs again, how does government find the revenues to maintain the social and physical infrastructure? How does government find ways to maintain a proportion of its population for some period of time, perhaps in the form of a type of income support or guaranteed annual income?

While there are few kudos for proposing a new tax, we feel the time has arrived to come to terms with changing economic conditions. We think that with the move to a new economy should come careful consideration of the adoption of a new tax base, one that is growing, one that is at the heart of the new economy. The base ought to be easily identified. Collection of the tax should not involve the creation of a large and costly bureaucracy. In short, the tax must be easy to collect and difficult to avoid.

In Adam Smith's time, the wealth of nations was a function of the division of labour and the extent of the market. Today the new wealth of nations is a function of information and communications technologies. The trillions of digital bits of information pulsing through global networks are the physical/electronic manifestation of the many transactions, conversations, voice and video messages, and programs that, taken together, make up the raw material of the new economy. This new national resource is a vital underpinning of the new economy – the new wealth of nations. It is important that the new wealth be accessible by governments, so that government can perform its traditional functions, so that the advanced countries can maintain hard-won standards of living, and so that the less-developed countries can advance and grow as well.

The new tax base is that myriad of transactions, images, voice, text, and data – all carried over global telecommunication, cable, and satellite networks. Just as the old economy could be found in railway freight cars and in 18-wheeler trucks, so too can the new wealth be found "riding" the flow of digital information, pulsing through the networks, 24 hours a day, every day. Just as some of the old tax base came from taxes on goods and transportation vehicles moving on the nation's rail lines and highways, so too can the new tax be found in the new distribution system of the new economy: the networks of the new economy.

Taxing the new wealth

James Tobin, the 1981 Nobel Prize-winning economist from Yale University, has proposed a tax on foreign exchange transactions which, he believes, would contribute to international policy coordination and needed autonomy on national monetary policies.[19] The present regime, which he describes as "dirty floating," involves occasional interventions by governments in the exchange rates of their currencies, without concern for the effect they may have on other nations. This, he contends, encourages speculation by traders based on short-term rather than long-term considerations, thus wasting "vast resources of intelligence and enterprise."

Tobin estimates that such transactions worth more than 100 billion dollars a day occur in New York alone. A 1 per cent tax would generate a billion dollars per working day, which Tobin suggested might appropriately go to international institutions such as the United Nations or the World Bank.

Roy Culpepper, the vice-president of the North-South Institute, in a *Financial Post* article[20] took Tobin's argument a step further. He stated that transactions worth about 1 trillion U.S. dollars take place daily on the world's currency markets. He suggested a more modest average ½ per cent tax on the face value of foreign exchange transactions. This, he says, would generate some 5 billion dollars daily, of which Canada's share might amount to some 35 billion dollars yearly - enough to wipe out the federal deficit.

Tobin's and Culpepper's arguments would not be possible if it were not for the enormous changes in global financial markets as a result of the advances in communications technology. Globalization has undermined many traditional tax bases, such as succession duties, corporation taxes, and income taxes for the very rich, since capital can be moved so easily to seek venues which maximize profitability, either because of local tax policies or other financial incentives.

Some of these incentives relate to labour costs and less stringent environmental regulatory requirements. If the improved technology is to benefit the many rather than the few, new forms of taxation will have to be exchanged for the old. An example we have often used is the automated teller machines (ATMs). Formerly, human beings provided the service and paid taxes on the salaries they earned. The new replacements, at present, have no such obligation and hence governments lose needed revenue and eventually raise the taxes of those who continue to be employed or find other kinds of assessment. The growing reliance on sales taxes is a case in point.

ATMs continue to increase in number. Virtually every bank or bank branch has its own, usually connected to one of the international networks such as Interac, Cirrus, Circuit, and Plus. At last count, in Canada alone, Interac estimated it was served by over 15,000 terminals, and approximately one billion dollars in transactions were processed annually using close to 30 million cards in the hands of consumers. A conservative estimate based on comparative population figures would place the U.S. figures at ten times that of Canada, that is, 150,000 terminals, 10 billion dollars in transactions and 300 million cards.

In addition to the services described in a previous paper,[21] the Royal Bank of Canada introduced in 1994 a voice-prompted telephone banking service named "Royal Direct," which permits any individual with an account at any of their multitude of branches to do virtually all of their banking business, 24 hours a day, from any phone in Canada or the U.S., using a toll-free number. The customer is provided with a personal access card containing a confidential access code and a special number to confirm bill payments and transfers between accounts for a cost of just $2.95 a month. The service enables clients to: pay monthly bills for gas, hydro, electricity, telephone, cable TV, credit and department store cards, and taxes; check the balance of personal or Visa accounts, transfer funds between personal accounts, shop and pay cash at retail stores by having the funds transferred from their personal bank account to the store in question, check current interest rates on loans, mortgages, and investments, as well as foreign currency exchange rates; receive up-to-date information on account activity; report lost or stolen Royal Bank client or Visa cards; apply for car loans, mortgages, et cetera; invest in associated mutual funds and receive a variety of other information.

Banking is only part of the story. The entertainment industry is also being captured by the media giants. Cable TV has been around for years in North America whereas direct broadcast satellites (DBS) have dominated Europe and Japan. Now the two modes seem to be converging as the use of cable is increasing in Europe and DBS systems are being introduced in the U.S. and Canada. Furthermore, the telephone giants are now eyeing what promises to be an increasingly profitable market in interactive services to the home, including conventional information services and networks, video games, and instantaneous. access (for a price) to the huge film libraries of the major Hollywood studios such as Time Warner Incorporated of New York.

Fibre optics, with a huge bandwidth capacity, is becoming the preferred technological carrier that will not only provide for the above services but will also permit the realization of the promise of high-definition television (HDTV) to not only provide cinema-quality pictures in the home but also to make electronic delivery to the home of any number of the world's preeminent newspapers. HDTV, combined with the interactive telephone service, is expected to revolutionize shopping patterns as any number of supermarkets and department stores will be only a few digitalized codes away and arrangements for either a pick up or home delivery a matter of personal choice.

The ability to create the impression of three-dimensional images has led to the expression "virtual reality." The fact that virtual reality is not real, but only a created effect, albeit a powerful one, is disturbing. The concern is that this very sophisticated technology will lead to dangerous concentrations of power in the commercial world. It is, indeed, a valid concern and needs to be addressed. Television in its present form has been accused by some of its critics of brainwashing viewers and unfairly skewing public opinion. As a result, regulatory agencies such as the FCC in the United States and the CRTC in Canada have set up rules to attempt to ensure that sponsors of commercials do not misrepresent their products; some schools of journalism and communications offer courses designed to improve the critical ability of their students. But it is obvious that a much greater effort is required to ensure that the general public is protected from abuses and, as far as possible, is aware of the techniques involved in creating the virtual reality images to which they are exposed, which should make viewers and hence is justifiably sceptical of what they see on their screens.

Many of the predicted information superhighways or, to use the current vernacular, infobahns, are already in place. In a very real sense their construction is comparable to the development of the network of expressways fifty years ago. Information is already available on demand, using the plethora of databases currently available to anyone with an inexpensive computer equipped with a modem and telephone. The same equipment can substitute for fax systems without the special equipment currently required. Interactive systems are now readily available and as the equipment becomes more and more user friendly the number of consumers will increase accordingly. As telephone companies become involved in the content game, whether it be information or entertainment, the use of the infobahns will grow geometrically. Teleshopping, movies on demand, email, and voice-response systems are only a sample of the services that will be in demand.

The traffic is already immense. During peak periods in North America, one trillion bits per second are transferred on the telephone networks. When these networks complete the transition from twisted copper wire cables to fibre optics the capacity will be able to expand to a peta bit per second, where peta stands for 10 to the 18th, or 1,000,000,000,000,000,000 bits per second.

Facsimile systems have been taking over from first-class mail, email systems are taking over from faxes, and funds are now more and more being transferred electronically. For example, the local and long distance revenues of Bell Canada amounted to 6.35 billion dollars in 1991. This is only a fraction of the returns possible as the new services become available to the general population and are not restricted to large businesses with expensive equipment and specially designed software. When all these applications are added to the automated teller example, the amounts will inevitably be greater than those perceived by Tobin and Culpepper.

What then does this all mean? Certainly as more and more services become automated, the demand for individual workers in the affected fields will decrease. The best guess from most economists is that while there may well be future long-term gains, there will inevitably be short-term pain. The questions we raise relate to the length of the short-term pain which is likely to be longer rather than shorter, and the degree to which such pain, long or short, is necessary in an age of rapid technological advancement. These queries will be addressed in the following sections, but first we believe it necessary to look at the financial dimensions of the changes to see if some innovative approaches to taxation policies might contribute to the realization of the new wealth of nations for the betterment of the lives of people in all walks of life.

It is our contention that a new economy is being created, and that new taxation policies should be designed that are appropriate for this new economy. Rather than being seen as a threat to living standards, the new technologies can be a bonanza. We currently have a taxation system in place appropriate to an industrial economy. We need to be creative. We need to develop new ways to get at the new wealth created by information technologies and distribute it more equitably. Improvements in economic efficiency should be reflected in higher, rather than lower, standards of living for all citizens in this era of the new wealth of nations. It is for this reason that we propose what we have termed a "bit tax" — a bit being the basic unit of the digital systems used by all modern computers and the growing proportion of all electronic transmissions. The justification for such a tax to replace or modify the majority of existing taxes is, we believe, compelling.

It would be simplistic in the extreme for two authors working with limited resources to analyze in any detail the impact in monetary terms of information and communications technology. Following any money trail is always exacting, but one that is as large and complex as the one we are discussing calls for the most careful, critical, and precise examination, using the most competent sources available; we do not have access to these sources, nor do we possess the supporting infrastructure to enable such a major study to be conducted.

But time is short and the need for solutions to the problems of insolvent governments and a confused and increasingly cynical populace has never been greater. We believe, as has been either stated or implied throughout this paper, that there are alternatives to simply following the status quo. It is our feeling, partly based on intuition, but also on studies we have made with respect to the automation of the workplace in general and the service sector in particular, that a new system of taxation is called for.

We believe that the examples already discussed in this section provide some support for the case we are attempting to make. Tobin and Culpepper argued for a small tax on foreign exchange. If we take Tobin's estimate that transactions amounting to about 100 billion U.S. dollars take place daily in New York alone, and assume an average tax of 1 per cent over a 250-working-day year, then the revenue from such a tax would amount to 250 billion U.S. dollars annually. If Culpepper is right and transactions on the world currency markets are 10 times that of New York, then the amount to be divided proportionally among the nations involved in these transactions would be 2.50 trillion U.S. dollars.

We used the ATM example to indicate how much money is transacted annually by consumers rather than businesses, who use the various systems provided by banks to transact much larger amounts of funds, since statistics regarding the amounts involved are not readily available. Following the same reasoning applied to the foreign exchange example, an additional trillion dollars could be accounted as new revenue. This amount obviously would be considerably higher if the features of the various systems, described in the earlier paper,[22] provided by the banks of the industrialized world were included, and the dollar amounts accounted for.

All of this does not touch the 10 to the 18th power bits per second passing through the infobahns. Multiply that by 60 x 60 x 24 x 365 and 6 more powers would have to be added. If there were to be a bit tax levied on the use of the infobahns at an annual rate of 10 to the minus 11th power, that is, 0.00000000001 cents per bit, it would produce a trillion dollars annually. But of course this is guess work. What the rate ought to be depends on many variables. Who bears the incidence of the tax? Can it be enacted by one country alone, or will it have to be done through international agreements? Which taxes will the bit tax replace? To find the answers to these and related questions, as we have said earlier, requires a major study, but it is a study that we are convinced will pay substantial dividends if it results in fresh approaches to meeting the challenge posed by the information revolution.

For the moment we think that we have made a sufficient case that a new tax is both necessary and feasible, and that the bit tax is an interesting approach. Further, by taxing bits, even by a very small amount, large amounts of revenues can be generated. We realize that implementation will take time and that studies must be made about where, and how, implementation takes place. Details are needed. But that type of study is one that can only be done by a group, one with a national or international mandate.

Some critics have said that the bit tax might slow the development of the information economy. Our reply has been: did the gasoline tax and vehicle license fees slow the development and diffusion of the automobile? Further dialogue has caused us to reflect on the possible need for special bit tax rates for very large bit packages. Downloading movies to the home will take very large quantities of bits, and charging the same rate is likely to impede the development of this activity. The bit tax rate for very large packages bears further research.

Further research is also needed on the impact of the bit tax. There is growing evidence that the productivity of ICT is greater than measured and that we are wealthier than we know how to measure, using measures of wealth and well-being designed for the industrial economy.[23]

If true, bringing in the bit tax might succeed in monetizing some of the uncounted or unappropriated productivity. A bit tax can lead to the monetization of some of the unappropriated productivity. One result: economic growth numbers will more accurately reflect the productivity advances brought by information technologies. And this new growth is likely to be noninflationary, since so much productivity has been unaccounted for. Some economists conclude that growth rates would be as much as a full percentage point higher if all productivity gains were accurately reflected in our national accounts.

A standard throw-away line is that "more research is needed." In this area of the monetization of productivity, it is clear that much, much more research is needed.

We also think that the actual mechanics of implementation will not be that difficult. We can measure bit streams in networks. So, given the necessary data, it should not be difficult to design an appropriate process. Software already exists that can perform this type of function. We are confident that system software can be designed to make the transfer of the funds accruing from a minuscule bit tax to wherever and to whomever the democratic will determines. By using the new tools to collect the taxes, as we shall see in subsequent sections, society will have in place a new source of revenues without the creation of an additional bureaucracy, and likely with the reduction of the existing one.

Bit tax: methodology

The concept of the bit tax has been explained in earlier chapters. Its focus is on adapting taxing methods to the new information society to provide tax revenues based on the wealth being generated by the integration of computers and communications, which are providing new, different, and obviously "here-to-stay" services to society.

The arguments proposed in the earlier sections demonstrate that a bit tax is a method that will offer a novel solution to provide for the needs of the emerging information society, and also to maintain an appropriate safety net by generating revenues based on an ICT paradigm. While the concept is appealing, often such ideas are dissipated when the "how-to" aspects are examined. This section proposes some ideas of how this bit tax might be implemented, and show that the approach is viable, both today and in the future.

The underlying logic of our proposed methodology[24] is that the bit tax be applied to the value-added addressable interactive digital services, described below, that are such a growing part of the information highway. The value that is added comes from interactivity. It is this value that provides the productivity in networks. Productivity and added value arise from the ability to interact with ICT systems: to browse, retrieve, transact and/or contribute information. Thus we suggest that all interactive digital information be subject to the new tax.

To implement the bit tax, a system that works directly with the ICT systems in place is proposed. Our proposed approach would also minimize the use of people and hence be a part of the information infrastructure in its own right. Using software, electronic security methods to ensure validity of the computation of the tax, and building on the monitoring and billing infrastructure already being installed by the various carriers and interactive service providers on the information highway, a simple, yet effective means of collecting the tax can be devised. This approach offers the potential of being a "smart" tax, allowing various elements of the ICT systems to be taxed at different rates to reflect the desires of society to provide a "just tax," if desired.

The information infrastructures now installed have three main elements: communications channels, information sources, and users. A unique feature of today's ICT systems is that the "user" can be either a person (or a group of people) or a computer (or groups of computers).

Information sources are most commonly people or on-line data bases available to the ICT system. Users access this information usually in a "search-and-retrieve" mode. Having the right information available at the right time is the key to the value that is added by using such systems, since delays in responding are minimized, and decisions can be made quickly. The communications channels can be local or long-distance. Business transactions flow over these channels, linking users and information sources in a way that allows organizations to respond more quickly to needs and to overcome the traditional delays inherent in handling information manually.

Communications channels usually "guide" signals via a "wire" (often called a "line" in telecommunications jargon). Communications channels can also "broadcast" signals from an antenna. Typical guided channels are copper wires, coaxial cables, cable-TV wires, phone wires, fibre channels, etc. Broadcast systems usually send a signal to a very broad area, in theory radiating signals from a central point in a spherical manner. In practice, most broadcast antennas have a pattern of broadcast that is designed to maximize coverage in specific areas. Satellite signals are also designed to cover specific areas.

Cable television is a special case. Currently cable television systems provide (mainly) a "broadcast" service over a "guided" communications channel. The originating signal is commonly a broadcast, received by the cable company over antennas, which then converts the signal to a form suitable for delivery to its customers over the "guided" cable system. Many cable companies have built their systems to be interactive in nature, such that a customer can request a service over the cable system via a "request" transaction and receive a service delivered just for that customer.[25]

A key concept in interactive systems is the need for the carrier of the information to know the specific location of the sender and receiver of the transactions in order to guide the signals between the two locations. In digital systems this is done by including a "header" message which includes the "addresses" of the sender and receiver. In the case of telephone systems, this address is simply the phone number of both parties. In the case of ATM systems, the address is a code denoting the physical location of the particular ATM machine, plus a code related to the account number of the user.

Broadcast systems do not have the name of the receiver in their signal, since they are broadcast equally to all parties. However, some broadcast systems (such as newspapers and television stations, which broadcast their signals via satellites to special receiving sites so that newspapers and newscasts are distributed at a more convenient time in various time zones of the coverage area) do include the receiving address in the header. Although these signals are considered to be "one-to-many" types of transactions, they are signals intended for users that are known to the carriers (satellites, microwave, or telecomm) who are able to track the transmission and charge their users for the service.

In the past few years, phone customers have seen the "distance" parameter in the charging algorithm reduced even further. In the U.S., for example, long-distance calls anywhere are charged by the minute, and not by distance. In Canada, the distance calling area for a fixed price is now becoming wider. Carriers now produce phone bills for customers computed to the nearest tenth of a minute, often including the exact time of the call, the calling number where the call originated, and the phone number called. One can anticipate that the carriers will soon be providing a new feature of printing bills with the names of the company/person called to make it easier, for companies in particular, to track call-usage patterns. With smart digital networks, there is now a logical connection between the name of the registered owner of a phone number and the number itself stored in central switches.

Interactive communications systems, particularly digitized systems, now have extremely sophisticated tracking software on the calls made and received by customers, including information on their duration (and often including the number of bits of information transmitted). Although this information generally only shows up as long-distance-call details on invoices, the information for local calls is also collected by the carriers, but not provided to those users who traditionally pay a flat monthly rate to the carriers for unlimited local service. Statistical information on local traffic trends is collected by the carriers for a specific purpose. This information on usage trends is needed to provide them with planning data so that they can anticipate when to upgrade their systems.

The sophistication in tracking calls and monitoring line usage by carriers is needed both to provide new services, as well as to bill users. And with the ability of users to select different long-distance carriers from a single terminal, as well as the interaction between different carriers worldwide to allow information transactions to be sent almost anywhere, the carriers have, of necessity, also worked out schemes for sharing the revenue amongst all the common carriers involved in handling the transmission of the signal so that the complexity is hidden from the user. This level of sophistication is handled totally by computer/communications systems in an automated manner, and monthly customer invoices are generated by computer without human intervention.

Interactivity is growing in ICT. For example, some traditional broadcast is already being replaced by programs on demand. As broadcasts move into a transaction mode, there is some value that is added to the user. Time shifting and getting the specific program or movie wanted from a very large, near-infinite menu is a valuable service that people are likely to want. Today's relatively clumsy video-on-demand will eventually evolve to a rather complex system characterized by users downloading the information to a special memory system at the user's location.

Companies with a large number of users of telecommunications often find that the costs of individual transactions (voice calls, or banks sending ATM messages, for example,) are expensive. A system has evolved over the years of allowing organizations with a very high volume of transactions to "lease" dedicated channels from carriers for a fixed monthly cost. Typically, this cost is anywhere from 35 to 70 percent of the cost of paying for transmissions on a "public" network where each transaction is billed. Almost all ATM services use such leased lines, as do many of the major companies that have a significant number of remote offices and a high information flow. Users will acquire these leased lines for many different purposes. Some might use them for guided broadcast transmission, others for extensive interactive transactions, such as credit cards and ATMs, or use in real-time inventory control. In either case the price is fixed, regardless of the content or level of usage of the leased channel. In deciding to adopt leased lines, customers will analyze their current costs and project the costs of leased lines to handle the traffic. Leased lines will often be adopted when the costs of the regular public lines are about 10 per cent more than the leased alternative.

At the core of our suggested methodology is a way of measuring the number of bits flowing over telecommunications lines. The bits are counted and there is no attempt made to gauge or get at the underlying value. Whether the bits refer to a million-dollar transaction or an email message, all bits are equal. All would be taxed equally.

For public long distance lines, the tax would apply to the actual information or flow of digital traffic. For leased lines, a fixed amount would be charged, based on the carrying capacity of the line measured in bits per second. Carriers would measure the local flow within a specified area. The local area could be an area code, a metro area, or a specified region. This measurement would produce a statistical average for the designated region – an amount that would represent the number of bits flowing in that area. This would provide the base rate of tax for that local area. Thus a very busy local area, however defined, would have a higher bit tax rate. Like high property taxes today, a high local bit tax rate might encourage new commercial ICT users to locate in areas where there is less traffic, where the bit taxes are relatively lower.

Hence, the implementation of the tax would fit into three broad categories:

1. Long-distance lines (general public), a variable tax directly proportional to the information flow between the major long-distance nodes in the country.
2. Leased lines (private lines), a fixed rate dependent on the bit-carrying capacity of the line.
3. Local traffic, a variable rated based on a statistical average of gross information flows captured at each local switch, using software already in place.

Certification of the software for measuring and computing the bit tax would need to be done by third parties, and a number of security controls would have to be put in place to provide the necessary assurances that the calculations meet the society's specifications and are not being subverted electronically. There may be instances where large corporations would set up their own private networks, acquiring the equipment independently of carriers. Normally these systems would have to be authorized by the appropriate regulatory agency. In reviewing such authorization, it would be feasible to charge a fixed amount of annual bit tax, based on the capacity of the channels being used.

The bit tax should be transparent to the user. The method proposed of rolling up measures of the information flow for a global summary for computation and presentation to the government of the revenues generated would make this approach generally transparent.

Although the approach recommended will make use of software tracking and information management systems already in place, by adding some computation algorithms, the approach may also need a bit-stream monitor system to compare the overall bit counts with the computed bit counts, for audit purposes. The carriers would install the appropriate software, in accordance with predefined security measures, and arrange to transfer the funds derived to the government. In return they would be paid for transferring funds. Since this will all be done with software anyway, with summary statements also being done by software, and probably with computer transactions moving the information (and even the funds) to governments electronically, the overall ongoing cost would be low (though there may be an initial set-up cost).

The system will be automatic, so much so that there will need to be special security monitors (also electronic) to ensure that the tax rate (the multiplying factor) has not been modified by either the carrier or the government without authorization from the political or electoral process.

As noted, the bit tax will be transparent. It will be something metred "out there" and remitted to governments. It will vary with the collective usage of networks. Use of the system by any one individual will not affect the amount of the taxes being collected. Depending on the state of profits, productivity, and competition, the taxes will be borne by the carriers or the users. It is likely that the tax burden or incidence will affect both carriers and users in varying degrees, depending on circumstances. At the micro level, the level of the final consumer, the bit tax would show up as an addition to the bill of users of ICT.

We have proposed a method or a way of applying the bit tax to interactive digital services. It is just one way; we are certain that others can be devised. In providing a methodology, we aren't trying to show the way, rather we are seeking to show that the technology is currently available to make collection of a bit tax relatively simple. In short, we trust that we have demonstrated, at least from a technical perspective, that the bit tax is a viable idea.

Concentrating on the digital bit stream at all levels of the ICT infrastructure is a way of getting at the productivity inherent in networks. It is important that the bit tax not be perceived as a user-pay tax. The information economy is just beginning its growth. We are against anything that would inhibit the development of the information economy – a user-pay charge could prove to be just such an inhibition. Thus we suggest that an average of digital traffic measured by region (area code, metro area, province or state, or nation) be collected for local traffic. This statistical average would provide the basis for bit taxes at the local level. Leased lines would pay some percentage of the carrying capacity of the line, while long distance public lines would be metred by usage patterns.

We are encouraged by the relative simplicity of our proposed system. Automatic collection of taxes, distributed automatically to the appropriate government – all put in place by building on the software already being operated by the carriers. A well-defined tax base, one that is growing. A tax that can be collected cheaply and simply. A system that can have very high safeguards to ensure system integrity.

Because the bit tax will be put in place on global networks, it is likely that implementation, at least in the early stages, will be among the G-7 countries or the member countries of the OECD.

Appropriate revenue-sharing arrangements will have to be put in place to ensure equitable distribution of the bit taxes. Here too, there is software already in place that can be used. The software that compensates country carriers in international telecommunications can be used in the area of bit taxes as well to make sure that revenues are shared in an equitable way between countries.

The bit tax is a viable idea. It is do-able from a technical point of view. Barriers to implementation will not come from the technical side. Our concern is that barriers might arise because "it's never been done before." Barriers to implementation might come as well from those who manage national and international fiscal accounts and are not aware of the changes wrought by the information economy. These economic changes that are so fundamental that the tax system of the industrial era is no longer adequate.

Putting aside doubts for the moment, it is clear that a bit tax would be a powerful generator of revenues that are badly needed in a time of transition. The new taxes could be introduced as some of the older taxes of the industrial era are wound down.

The new wealth created by ICT provides new opportunities for all countries. The old tax base can, over time, be replaced by a tax base that is more appropriate for the new economy. But the new wealth can be used for broader purposes. It can be used to repair some of the damage caused by costs of growth in the industrial era. The new wealth can be used for a range of public investments. We turn now to some ways in which the new revenues from a new tax base can truly contribute to the wealth of nations.

What to do with the new revenues: one proposal

It is apparent that substantial revenues will accrue from the combination of the bit tax described above and the "speculators' tax," as proposed by Nobel prize-winner James Tobin and expanded by Roy Culpepper in his piece in the 6 July 1994 edition of the *Financial Post*.

One critic, a former justice of British Columbia's Supreme Court, worried that "Glutinous governments will collect the fees – but channel them into more follies, more entitlements, et cetera."[26] This is a natural concern and one that must be dealt with. The intent of this book is not to advocate pouring money into bureaucratic coffers but to find a solution to the structural unemployment faced by so many people in a period graced by a benign new technology, and to use the benefits to improve the quality of life of the billions struggling for existence on a planet beset with a plethora of problems ranging from mounting public debt and a frightening escalation of violent crime and terrorism to a deteriorating environment, which threatens the survival of life itself.

It is also hoped that the inability of virtually all governments to discharge their obligations to their citizens, while under pressure from the global marketplace to remain solvent, can be addressed by getting rid of an archaic tax system based on principles developed during the Industrial Revolution and replacing it with one more in tune with the information age. The old system is slowly strangling the highly motivated and productive middle classes and, while favouring an elite few, cannot cope with the plight of the ever-increasing poor.

It is easy enough to cry, "Make the unemployed work for their welfare cheques and they will soon find real jobs." What kind of work is the question. One former resident of a communist country referred to what he called "dummy buttons." These were buttons and gadgets attached to dials. But the dials were spurious and changed nothing. They were meant only to keep the workers busy. What a travesty when there is so much real work that needs to be done! The list of problems seems endless. Lakes, rivers, oceans, and the air we breathe are subject to increasing pollution. Health-care systems are facing cutbacks that can only grow more serious as demographic changes reflect an aging population. The concept of equal educational opportunities is coming under review. The principle of universality, so long considered a linchpin of democracies, is more and more being questioned.

There are, indeed, many essential jobs to be done if only there were the funds available to pay for them.

One example relates to the depletion of the earth's ozone layer. An article on cutaneous melanoma in *The New England Journal* of *Medicine*[27] stated that the incidence has almost tripled in the past four decades, growing faster than that of any other cancer, and projected that by the year 2000 almost one per cent of the population of the United States would be affected. In looking to causes, the author referred to the depletion of the earth's ozone layer, believed to be induced by artificial chlorofluorocarbons (CFCs). It is plain that emissions of these and other manufactured aerosol compounds must be reduced. But the cost of doing so is enormous.

North American society, in particular, has become addicted to electric refrigerators and freezers, together with air-conditioned cars, homes, and places of work. Many of our appliances use freon as a cooling agent. Converting the offending units to more benign components would not only protect future generations but would also mean work for manufacturers and their employees.

Although not all scientist are convinced that freon in its present form presents the threat to the atmosphere that was at one time believed, there is no doubt about the need to reduce the emissions of sulphur and carbon dioxide. These industrial gases that humans are releasing constitute a very real and present danger to the biosphere. As an article in *Scientific American*[28] observed, human activity produces more than two-thirds of the troposphere's supply of sulphur gases, and about 90 per cent of that is created in the Northern Hemisphere. The cost of finding and developing industrial substitutes will require not only ingenuity but substantial funds as well. The article concluded: "The longer the world delays implicating reduction the more severe will be the consequences."

Just as it took the industrial demands associated with the Second World War to finally bring us out of the economic effects of the depression of the 1930s, the work associated with protecting the ozone layer and other remedial environmental projects could do the same today, but with a constructive objective rather than the creation of instruments of war.

Precedents exist for the use of public money to pay consumer costs related to massive changeovers as a result of advances in technology. In the early developments of electricity on the North

American continent, many frequencies were used, ranging from 16⅔ to 133 cycles. In time, 60 cycles became standard for utility services. The Niagara-Hudson system, which served a large part of Ontario, had settled on 25 cycles, which had certain advantages for rotary-style converters. However, with growth in demand for lighting and other electric devices, 60-cycle systems provided significant benefits while mercury rectifiers had practically replaced rotary converters.

In 1947 the decision was taken by the Hydro-Electric Power Commission of Ontario to appoint the U.S. firm, Stone and Webster Engineering Corporation, to provide a report on the advisability of changing the frequency of the Commission's 25 cycle system to 60 cycles and to estimate the costs involved. The lengthy study (150+ pages) recommended that the conversion program be adopted and started as quickly as possible. Gross costs were deemed to be approximately $190,000,000 in 1947 dollars, and provided for consumers to be able to interchange frequency-sensitive equipment freely in the new 60-cycle areas. Appliances listed included: clocks, fans, furnace blowers, hair dryers, humidifiers, electric irons, utility and hobby motors, oil burners, radios, ranges, record players, sealed and open refrigerator units, sun lamps, vacuum cleaners, and washing machines.

Supported by two subsequent reports from Clarkson, Gordon & Company, and Harold Hobson, the Commission decided to accept the recommendations, and after the appropriate legislation was passed in the Ontario Legislature the conversion process began. In Toronto the first customer to receive the changeover was the Toronto Transportation Commission's Beaches station in 1949. On 7 March 1955, the standardization of customers' equipment began. By July 1959 the program was completed. In just over four years, 205,195 customers had been switched over.[29] It was a massive undertaking funded with public money and carried out by firms in the private sector. The result was a much-improved system that brought substantial savings in the long run. The consultants had predicted that the entire cost would be recovered by 1964. It is likely that, given the enormous growth in the demand for power, their estimate was conservative.

Just as there is no shortage of problems, there is also no shortage of opportunities. In his 1992 report to the Interaction Council,[30] Helmut Schmidt, the former German chancellor, declared that the world is at a crucial turning point. Among the issues he addressed were: instabilities arising from the political changes taking place in Eastern Europe, in particular the dispersion of clandestine nuclear weapons; the linkage of a global population explosion and an ecological burnout; the overriding problem of nuclear waste disposal, and the reduction of CO_2 through the development of nonrenewable energy sources, including biomass, wind, and solar.

All the issues Schmidt listed are valid, but appropriate action involves work of one kind or another. Political commitment is a must, as are the necessary intellectual and financial resources. The new information technologies are invaluable assets. They have the capacity to marshal data on a worldwide basis and assist in calculating and assessing the relative effectiveness of various proposals. As we have seen, these new technologies, associated with a bit tax of one form or another, can also be the source of the funds that will be required to implement whatever strategy and procedure is approved.

Conclusion

The challenge of large-scale and apparently structural unemployment in a period of increasing productivity, together with a declining tax base, has influenced the subject matter of both this book and the paper that preceeded it, "The New Tools,"[31] written two years earlier. As we said then, "the relative newness of the computerization of society has caught all of us, including governments and private corporations, off guard."

Uncertainty with regard to the future, combined with mounting international competition have, in this age of information, left politicians and the public alike with misgivings they find difficult to articulate. The result has been a public policy vacuum in which the only answer is presumed to lie in the reduction of government spending, even at the cost of cutting services such as education and health care that have always been the symbols of enlightenment associated with democratic systems.

It is in the context of social sustainability that we present the ideas in this book. By this we mean sustaining economic development; sustaining the capacity for effective governance; and sustaining the conditions for maintaining democracy in Canada.

If we do not maintain effective demand in the economy, then we will be facing a recession or worse. If governments in Canada do not receive sufficient tax revenues to maintain our social and physical infrastructure and to provide a range of public goods, then the capacity to govern effectively is diminished. If we do not provide income to those whose skills are no longer needed in the information economy, then we are sure to see the development of a two-tier society. A two-tier society, we believe, poses a threat to democracy as we have known it in Canada.

As indicated earlier, the problem does not lie in our ability to produce. Nor does it lie in a lack of material resources. The technological tools currently at our disposal enable us to produce enough to generate sufficient income to solve most, if not all, of our economic problems. It also does not lie in any lack of work that needs to be done. Coping with global warming, ozone depletion, the spread of violence, the needs of an aging population, the alleviation of poverty, and the elimination of nuclear, chemical, and biological weapons all require new and additional forms of human endeavour. As the Interaction Council pointed out, "the world economy faces a daunting agenda for action ... and all these challenges call for substantive funds." Sadly, we seem to be dealing with nation-states that have lost their way: a failure of imagination coupled with a failure of will.

The challenge is to locate and access these resources in a time when television images speak of untold riches and commentators in the press write about deficits and insolvent governments. We believe the riches are there and agree that most governments are insolvent. The dilemma is how to resolve the two conditions; how to tap the productivity of the new factor of production – information technology. How to convince governments to adopt a policy agenda more in keeping with the New Economy, one that is capable of generating the needed fiscal resources to deal with a work force and workplace that are being buffeted by the twin forces of globalization and information technology.

Information is a true element of production: it can be in the form of entertainment, such as movies and video games; in the form of financial management, such as electronic data interchange systems for businesses and automatic tellers for the average citizen; in systems designed to control aircraft traffic in the skies and baggage distribution on the ground below; and in managing the maze of telephone calls, faxes, email and charge-card accounts that characterize life in this latter part of the twentieth century.

Hardware and software developments are changing the world at a pace never before imagined. Multinational corporations have acquired independence and power never dreamed of by their counterparts such as the East India and Hudson's Bay companies in a previous era, nor by giants such as Carnegie, Ford, and Rockefeller not so many decades ago. Globalization has meant that for the mega-enterprise, we live in a borderless world where services flow between countries linked by real time networks involving every form of information technology regardless of many of the so-called national interests.

The wealth is there. Whether it is in the traffic on the various electronic highways or in the content that is carried on them, it is there. The problem is to find the method by which human needs and wants can be met in this changing economic environment.

We have used the term "bit tax" because the bit is the symbol of the digitalized world in which we live. Whether the tax is levied on the traffic carried by the fibre optic cable and the microwave paths, or whether it is levied on the content, such as the trillion dollars per day on the foreign exchange markets of the world, or on a combination of the two, it is the only gateway into the wealth that is being generated in this age of information.

The solution to us seems clear. In Tennyson's words, "Ring out the old, ring in the new." Get rid of antiquated taxes that no longer are able to relate to the new wealth of nations and bring in innovative tariffs that will take the load off the overburdened shoulders of individuals and place it on the much more impersonal robotic-like shoulders of the engine of wealth that is the feature of the end of the old millennium and the beginning of the new.

There is a particular urgency connected with our recommendation. Business as usual, as we pointed out in the earlier paper, "The New Tools," is not an option. In North America, economies are experiencing overall growth, while the average household faces a decline in income. This is a far from healthy phenomenon in governments, where the sovereign power rests with the people. Inevitably, if it is left to continue, drastic solutions will begin to become attractive and the electorate will opt for a charlatan who promises to right wrongs whether these wrongs be real or imagined.

In his article "Workers and the World Economy," in *Foreign Affairs* (May/June 1996), Ethan B. Kapstein sends an alarm to the world policy community. "The world may be moving inexorably toward one of those tragic moments that will lead future historians to ask, why was nothing done in time? Were the economic and policy elites unaware of the profound disruption that economic and technological change were causing working men and women? What prevented them from taking the steps necessary to prevent a global social crisis?" It is in this spirit that we present the analysis and ideas in this book.

Unhappily, there is much to be done before the concept we have proposed can be elaborated on to be able to stand the test of the questions that those committed to the status quo are bound to raise. Good research regarding the technical issues and the underlying economics of the distribution of the new wealth of nations is essential. The transition from traditional methods of taxation to deductions from the source of activity will be far from easy. Although it would not be necessary to obtain agreement from all the nation-states, no one country could adopt such a major policy by itself. This raises the question of broad agreement among the major nations: tax havens will surely appear, but can their impact be minimized? It stands to reason that agreement from the major trading partners would have to be reached, and further, that reasonably common rates of taxation would have to apply.

It is our hope that a major study will be mounted under the auspices of an organization with impeccable qualifications and will involve individuals representative of a variety of jurisdictions. It is only through such a process that we can envisage a successful resolution to the tremendous challenges facing democracies in the coming century.

Notes

1. Thomas H. McCraw, "The Trouble with Adam Smith," *The American Scholar*, Summer 1992, Phi Beta Kappa Society, Washington, DC.
2. Nicholas Chamie, "Why the Jobless Recovery: Youth Abandon Labour Market," Conference Board of Canada, September 1995.
3. Joan Palevsky, "Nationalism and the Politics of Resentment," *The American Scholar*, Summer 1994, Phi Beta Kappa Society, Washington, DC.
4. Mary Augustine, "And Man Created...," *Development Forum* (New York: United Nations Information Committee, 1988).
5. Willy Brandt, *World Armament and World Hunger*, (London: Victor Gollancz, 1986).
6. The data was taken from various articles in *The New York Times, The Globe and Mail*, and David P. Ross, "Work and Income Security in the Nineties," *Canadian Council on Social Development Report* (Ottawa: Canadian Council on Social Development, 1987).
7. Joann S. Lublin, "The Great Divide: CEO pay keeps soaring leaving everybody else further and further behind," *Wall Street Journal*, 11 April 1996.
8. T. Ran Ide and Arthur J. Cordell, "The New Tools: Implications for the Future of Work," *Shifting Time: Social Policy and the Future of Work* (Toronto: Between the Lines, 1994).
9. Linda Diebel, *Toronto Star*, 6 November 1994.
10. Eleanora Masini, "Needs and Dynamics," *Human Needs*, K. Lederer, ed. (Konestein: Verlaj Anton Hain, 1980).
11. Diana Malpede, in Rio-Creteil-Pekin, *Femmes et Changements*, 1994.
12. A.H. Maslow, "A Theory of Human Motivation," *Psychological Review*, 1943.

13. John McHale and Magda Cordell McHale, *Basic Human Needs* (New Brunswick, N.J.: Transaction Books, 1977).
14. Rick Salutin, *The Globe and Mail*, 4 November 1994.
15. McCraw, "The Trouble with Adam Smith."
16. *The Canadian Information Highway: Building Canada's Information and Communications Infrastructure*, a discussion paper of Industry Canada (Ottawa: Government of Canada, 1994), pp. 3-4.
17. *The Economist*, "Survey of the World Economy," 28 September 1996, p. 4.
18. Ide and Cordell, "The New Tools."
19. James Tobin, "Speculators' Tax" in *New Economy* (Fort Worth, TX: The Dryden Press, 1994).
20. Roy Culpepper, *The Financial Post*, 6 July 1994, Toronto.
21. Ide and Cordell, "The New Tools."
22. Ibid.
23. See Leonard I. Nakamura, "Is U.S. Economic Performance Really That Bad?" Working Paper No. 95-21, Federal Reserve Bank of Philadelphia, October 1995. Nakamura suggests that quality increases are not reflected in the price of products; that productivity is greater than measured; that true output is greater than measured by up to 40 percent. See also *The Economist* survey, "The World Economy," 28 September 1996. Among the many reasons offered for why productivity is not rising, the publication suggests that our measuring tools are obsolete. "The tools used for measuring productivity are more suited to the output of 19th century dark satanic mills than 21st century electronic wizardry."
24. An important background paper was prepared for the authors by Dr. A. Ronald Elliott of Ottawa, Canada, an expert in digital communications. Selected excerpts make up the substance of this section.
25. Traditionally, transactions have been considered to be relatively short messages. The term has been used mainly to describe systems that have many users linked to a large central data-base such as on-line banking systems, or airline reservation systems, etc. However, the term is slowly changing to mean any message sent to or from a user/source of information, as the messages become digital in nature. As a result, long messages consisting of perhaps several minutes of a video can be considered to be a transaction message.

26. In a private communication to T. Ran Ide, January 1994.
27. Howard K. Koh, "Cutaneous Melanoma," *The New England Journal of Medicine*, 18 July 1991.
28. Charlson and Wigley, "Sulfate Aerosol and Climate Change," *Scientific American*, February 1994.
29. Information has been obtained from the 75th Anniversary Annual Report of Toronto Hydro (1985) and reports filed with the Hydro-Electric Power Commission of Ontario by: Stone and Webster Engineering Corporation, Clarkson, Gordon & Company, and Harold Hobson. (Toronto: Ontario Hydro Public Reference Centre, 1947).
30. Helmut Schmidt, "The Search for Global Order: The Problem of Survival," *Interaction Council*, April 1993.
31. Ide and Cordell, "The New Tools."

three

the bit tax
taxing value in the emerging information society

luc soete & karin kamp

Introduction*

The report "Building the European Information Society for Us All" – a "first reflections" report of an independent group of experts[1] established by the European Commission to advise on the social and societal aspects of the information society – contains a recommendation for the investigation of "appropriate ways in which the benefits of the Information Society (IS) can be more equally distributed between those who benefit and those who lose. Such research should focus on practical, implementable policies at the European level, which do not jeopardizse the emergence of the IS. More specifically, the expert group would like the Commission to undertake research to find out whether a 'bit tax' might be a feasible tool in achieving such redistribution aims." Despite the prudence of the recommendation's language, the reference to the idea

---

* Parts of this article were first published in *Science and Public Policy*, Vol. 23, No. 6.

of a bit tax[2] has led to considerable reaction amongst the press, policymakers, and individual Internet users.[3] Such reactions range from immediate adherence and even proposals for implementation[4] to disbelief and disgust. As chairman of the so-called High Level Expert Group[5] and the person most eager to have this recommendation included in the report, the first author of this paper is particularly keen on elaborating on the idea of the bit tax, following the policy reaction and press reports regarding what has been called by some a new Loch Ness tax monster.[6]

Perhaps it is not surprising that in the present, global free market environment, any suggestion for a new tax is likely to be greeted with scepticism and to be quickly rejected. The fact that the first thing a group of "high level" experts on the Information Society would come up with is a tax on the transmission of information creates, understandably, some level of disbelief, particularly from those who have set their hopes for a renewed expansion of economic growth in Europe and elsewhere in the world on the current wave of new information and communication technologies.[7] More surprising though, in the case of the bit tax proposal, is that the simple recommendation to research the feasibility of such a new tax has been rejected by some at the outset, for fear that "it might give the wrong signal" to potential investors.[8] Less surprising are the extremely negative responses of individual Internet users. Those responses received thus far on email all fear the possible attempt of the state to tax both communication and freedom of speech. Finally, on the side of the technical experts, the reaction has also been, by and large, negative: "bits" are, or will soon be, an irrelevant measure of transmission intensity; bits are difficult if not impossible to monitor; "broadband" capacity is in effect infinite; etc.

Before being convinced by all these (too?) quick responses and foreclosing even the research option on the bit tax, we summarize briefly in these couple of pages the main arguments in favour of such a tax, and why it is, in our view at least, an essential part of the distributional challenges of the emerging information society.[9] By doing so, we put forward a highly personalized vision of the aim, nature, and possible uses of a bit tax. Let the traditional policy reader thus be warned: apart from a few papers by Cordell, there is virtually no literature on this subject. This is a "no-man's research land."[10] For this reason only the EU experts' group request for further research seems to be more than justified.

The aim: the "bit tax" as part of a shift in the tax base of society

The main economic argument for a bit tax is fairly straightforward. As our economy becomes more and more characterized by the production, distribution, and consumption of intangibles from an economy that was characterized by the production, distribution, and consumption of tangibles, it seems relevant to question whether or not the present tax base remains adequate. Historically, the goods we consumed were physical, and therefore the production, distribution, and consumption of these goods was easily taxable. The inputs required for production could be easily measured, the value-added generated through the whole industrial and distribution process easily traced, and the final consumption easily located. Today, as economic activity becomes increasingly concentrated in immaterial information transactions, large parts of these value chains appear invisible; so invisible that a substantial part evaporates, incorporated in material goods or services, in the end hidden in an unmeasured, but not unnoticed, increased consumer surplus.

These invisible gains are, as has been argued at length in the recent OECD report on Technology, Productivity and Job Creation, behind the so-called Solow paradox[11] – the fact that we do not seem to notice in official statistics the benefits of the new information and communication technologies. They are also, as increasingly acknowledged in the U.S.,[12] behind the significant "overestimation" of inflation in the official Consumer Price Index figures, whereby the growing consumer surplus associated with new and better goods and services have been systematically ignored. Hence, there is, as argued by Cordell, at least a suspicion that part of the productivity and consumer gains from the new information and communication technologies has disappeared into the production and distribution networks and has not been reflected in lower prices or higher profits or salaries.

At the same time, goods that were traditionally distributed physically are becoming increasingly available via the networks. The taxing of the distribution of these goods, which has traditionally formed one of the essential bases for national, state, or even local government's tax revenues is, as a result, eroding rapidly. It has been estimated that in the U.S. the use of the Internet by individual consumers accessing mail-order companies, exempt from sales taxes, has meant a reduction in state sales tax revenues of over $3 billion in 1995.[13]

More generally, it can be argued that the simple fact of not adjusting a nation's tax basis will automatically imply a nonneutrality of different distribution or communication systems, with the newest communication systems avoiding, either by accident or by design, the prevailing tax levying system. The difference between the United States' sales tax system and Europe's VAT system is illustrative in this regard. In the U.S., it is by and large accidental – i.e., the mail-order companies local sales tax exemption – that electronic systems are eroding local sales taxes. In Europe it is the levying of VAT on services (banking, insurance, telephone, etc.) which is increasingly avoided because of the global access and footloose location possibilities of such service providers through Internet. At the same time, providers of goods and services using traditional means become less competitive since they must pay taxes on their visible and easily traceable goods or services. Send a letter through the post or special delivery and tax will be paid on the stamp or delivery bill; make a telephone call and – at least in Europe – VAT will be levied on the phone bill; order the experts' group report "Building the European Information Society for Us All" from the EU and VAT will be paid on postal costs. Via electronic means, however, the tax rate on all these transactions is practically nil (with the exception of the VAT on the couple of seconds of dial-up and local telephone costs). Furthermore, since there will be less physical distribution of these goods, less revenues from sales or VAT taxes will be earned.[14] More generally, it can be stated that in the current configuration of governments' methods of raising revenues from the distribution of goods and services, electronic networks are likely to systematically lead to less tax being charged and collected.

It appears that in recent months, since this paper was first circulated, this issue has gained significant attention in both the United States and the EU. Apparently, the European Commission is planning to implement a change in the application of VAT by having VAT charged based on the consumption point as opposed to the location of company headquarters. In other words, subscribers to online services such as AOL and CompuServe and to telephone call-back services who have been excluded from paying VAT because the companies are headquartered in the U.S., will, starting next year, have to pay VAT on these services.[15] In the U.S., the Interactive Services Association, a U.S.-based trade organization for the Internet and online industry, recently commissioned a taskforce to help policymakers at all levels of government understand the issues when they consider imposing taxes on Internet and online services. In the executive summary of their forthcoming White Paper, "Logging On to Cyberspace Tax Policy," the task force concluded that "the only type of tax that can be applied effectively to Internet and online transactions will be a transaction tax that is imposed upon the purchasers, not upon the Industry; that, in the absence of better information as to the location of the purchaser, a seller should be allowed to rely upon the billing address to identify the state whose tax will apply; and that the billed charges should be used to determine the amount of the end users' tax liability. New developments, such as the increasing use of electronic cash to pay billed charges can be expected to produce new tax collection and allocation challenges."[16]

The Department of the Treasury, the office of tax policy in the U.S., has recently expressed its interest in the tax policy implications of developments in communications technology and electronic commerce as well.[17] Their contribution is meant to reexamine the Internal Revenue Code and the generally accepted principles of international tax policy. It is a stepping stone in this reexamination process, encouraging the stimulation of public discussion and feedback by taxpayers, practitioners, academics, etc.

Furthermore, the Clinton administration has proposed declaring the Internet a global duty-free zone for goods and services that are bought and delivered electronically.[18] Apparently, the aim of the proposal is to ensure that Internet commerce is not "encumbered" by customs duties or any forms of taxation such as a bit tax. U.S. software producers are clearly delighted by the proposal. Reaction by local state governments and other countries however, is expected to be less favourable, as they fear that electronic commerce will erode their revenue base.

The main economic argument for a shift in the tax base away from tangibles towards intangibles is simple. Just as one to two hundred years ago economic discussions were dominated by the "corn tax," reflecting the importance of grain for the national economy, today the dominant issue should be how governments can adjust their tax base in line with the changing economic structure towards an information society and the increasing importance of information transmission for economic production and consumption. Shifting tax revenues on the basis of a tax on the individual electronic "bits" or "bytes" appears from the outset the most straightforward and logical taxing method. As Cordell puts it: "The new wealth of nations is to be found in the trillions of digital bits of information pulsing through global networks. These are the physical/electrical manifestation of the many transactions, conversations, voice and video messages and programs that, taken together, record the process of production, distribution, and consumption in the new economy....The value that is added comes from interactivity. It is this value that provides the productivity in networks."[19] The analogy between taxes on "motor highways" and "information highways" is from this perspective illustrative. As in the case of the automobile, gasoline or bridge taxes are being paid on physical highways, where on the information superhighway digital traffic is being taxed per bit.

On the nature of the "bit tax": from taxing value added to taxing transmission

As mentioned above, the main consumption/production tax levied in the EU countries is the Value Added Tax (VAT). The latter provides an increasingly harmonized tax base for the individual member countries, and allows goods and services to be taxed at their various points of production and value-added creation. A VAT system is ideal in the case of material goods or services being produced. The "value-added" contributions of the various intermediary inputs are easily quantifiable, the value of the final good or service consisting in a relatively straightforward manner of the amalgamation of these various inputs.

In the case of information and communication services, it is very difficult to talk in any real or meaningful way about a tax on "value added." Taxing the value added of a telephone conversation by levying a certain tax percentage on the bill of a telephone call has little meaning to it. The cost of the communication will have no relationship to the possible value of the communication, but rather be a function of the distance (local/long distance) and time (seconds/minutes) of the communication.

We propose that the bit tax fits within a broader idea to replace value-added tax-based systems on immaterial goods and services with a transmission-based tax system, i.e., a system by which the tax is levied as a proportion of the "intensity" of the information or communication transmission. The number of bits or bytes is considered as a more representative unit to provide an indication of such transmission intensity than time or distance would be. Only in the case of communication systems using a constant number of bits per second, such as a telephone conversation, will there be a straightforward relation between time and transmission intensity.

In other words, a bit tax would not be related in any direct way to the actual "value" of a communication, rather it would focus on the transmission of information. From this perspective it is the number of bits that "count," whether transmitted at a constant rate over time as in a telephone communication or in packages over the broadband as on Internet. In practical terms a bit tax proposal would thus involve the introduction of "bit measuring" equipment on all communication equipment (similar to the case of electricity metres),[20] thus enabling consumers and users to monitor the volume of bits, whether they are transmitted by line or satellite. It would make no difference if a user accessed an email message from a friend or a huge financial transaction. The amount paid would only be based on the number of bits transmitted.

The amount would be kept very low – Cordell proposed a tax of .000001 cents/bit[21] (or one cent per megabit) – without anybody really knowing what the effect of this would be in terms of total government revenue or individual user or company cost. In a recent intervention at a conference on teleworking, the Belgian Minister for Telecommunications Di Rupo referred to a total figure of 10^{18} bits being transmitted in and out of Belgium. At the Cordell rate, this would imply a substantial amount of additional government tax revenues: some $10 billion, or some 4 per cent of Belgium's GDP. At a recent data base conference, Lewis Platt, CEO and Chairman of Hewlett-Packard, indicated that HP currently uses its intranet main backbone at a rate of some 5 terabytes a month (or 480 terabits a year). Assume for a moment that these intranet bits could be monitored: this would imply that HP would pay a total bit tax bill of some $4.8 million on total worldwide revenues for HP in 1995 of some $32 billion and profits of some $5 billion. In other words, a tax bill of less than .1 per cent of current profits. What a bit tax would amount to with respect to individual users is more difficult to calculate, even though the surfing or transferring of particular sets of information can easily be calculated. Many individual users may be happy to know, for example, that the bit tax cost for down loading Pamela Anderson's latest swimsuit pose would be less than half a cent.

However, a more pragmatic method more in line with the idea of the bit tax replacing all VAT on information and communication services might imply the identification of a tax rate level per bit that would be more or less equivalent to the total VAT cost on an average user's telephone bill. This way one might avoid some of the much exaggerated negative reactions[22] on the possible negative impact a bit tax might have on the future development of "call centres" and other new information-service-based activities popular in many of the regional European development plans, and looked upon as the main new employment providers of the future.

But to discuss these as well as other practicalities amounts at this stage to not much more than speculation. We have not addressed *faute d'expertise*, the technical issues involved. Obviously, it is easy to dismiss the whole bit tax idea on technical grounds, whereby bits, for example, can no longer be monitored such as in the case of satellite communication. However, the argument for the use of bits is that they are a readily available electronic unit measure reflecting data or information transmission. Obviously alternative measures might be or become more appropriate than the bit as a taxing unit. The main point is that there surely is one measure that would give some indication of transmission intensity, even using satellite communication, and whose monitoring is relatively straightforward. Such measures might currently not be recorded, but as mentioned earlier, the bit tax proposal does involve the design of new measuring instruments to record and trace transmission intensity. While we agree with those who question whether or not the bit tax revenues would be sufficiently high so as to cover these accounting costs,[23] this is precisely what the proposed research will need to figure out. The literature on new and alternative methods of pricing information and communication services may be of relevance here. To some extent the whole notion of an alternative taxing of information services is part of the much broader discussion of how we should price information in our societies, and in particular the possible shift towards usage-based pricing.[24]

Besides addressing issues of technical feasibility, the proposed research on the bit tax should identify an "optimal" tax rate, the costs for the average individual user, for small and large companies, and the total amount of additional tax revenues for the government. Only when this is done can a real discussion take place on whether, and to what extent, the bit tax proposal is likely to have negative effects on competitiveness, future employment, inflation, delocalization, future use of the Internet, or even freedom of speech. To argue on a priori grounds that it will is foolish. To try to foreclose even the possibility of investigating the issue is even more foolish, and contrasts sharply with the creative challenges the Information Society is confronting us all with.

On possible additional benefits of the bit tax: reducing information pollution and congestion

Compared to other taxes, such as the eco CO_2-tax or even Tobin's "speculators' tax" proposal, taxing the transmission of information does not, at least at first sight, involve the pricing of any negative externality, rather the contrary. The substitution of physical transport of persons or goods for electronic information transmission (as in the case of teleworking or at least partly in the case of teleshopping) is likely to reduce substantially the negative environmental and congestion externalities of cheap transport and the dramatic increase in mobility typical of society's postwar industrial development growth path. Therefore, at first sight, a bit tax proposal is not justified on the basis of negative externalities.

However, a bit tax might reduce one negative externality of network technologies with low or zero marginal costs: the rapidly growing congestion and increasing amount of "junk" and irrelevant information being transmitted. Congestion has become more serious as users increasingly access colour images, sound files, and video – all with very high bandwidth applications. The increased number of users (in 1995 the Internet doubled in size, as it has done every year since 1988) adds to the congestion problem. Although technological developments will help to alleviate the problem, new subscribers, combined with increased usage of "taxing" multi-media applications, will also increase congestion. For this reason, there is general agreement amongst users as well as Internet experts that congestion will be an increasingly serious problem.

To address the congestion problem, some analysts have, actually, proposed setting up pricing schemes that charge based on usage.[25] The argument behind usage-based pricing starts from the assumption that even though bandwidth is continually increasing, Internet is a scarce resource and it is unlikely that it will be able to keep up with demand growth. As pointed out in Brody: "Congestion on the Internet is already hindering those that attempt to use applications during peak business hours.... The problem becomes particularly acute when some special event occurs. After the comet Shoemaker-Levy struck Jupiter, for example, and people downloaded the dramatic telescope images, large portions of the Internet slowed down. In such situations, urgent transmissions, such as a potentially lifesaving video conference between a surgeon and a radiologist, might queue up behind a home movie that someone put on the Net just for fun. In effect, the Net can be dominated by people with a lot of time on their hands, and there is no provision for buying one's way to the front of the line."[26] More generally, there is considerable agreement amongst analysts that some type of disincentive is required to curb Internet consumption.

The main economic problem is that there is no incentive to be "economical" with information, since the cost difference between sending 1 byte/second or 1 billion bytes/second is minimal, often close to zero. The opposite might actually be the case. As the High Level Expert Group report emphasized: "For us the distinctions between 'data', 'information' and 'knowledge' and between 'codified' and 'tacit' knowledge are of considerable importance. From our standpoint, the generation of unstructured data does not automatically lead to the creation of information, nor can all information be equated with knowledge. All information can be classified, analysed and reflected upon and otherwise processed to generate knowledge. Information, in our sense, is comparable to raw materials processed by industry to make useful products. One of the main effects of the new ICTs has been a billion-fold reduction in cost and speed of storing and transmitting information. However, such ICTs had no such effect on knowledge, still less on wisdom."[27] One of the main problems for the IS, therefore, is to develop the skills and tacit knowledge to make effective use of this vast resource. Without such tacit knowledge, to navigate the rough seas of on-line information, with its misinformation, poor quality information, unreliable information and advertising hype could induce nausea." [28]

The ease and low cost of accessing information has certainly been behind the dramatic growth in Internet, mobile, and other forms of electronic communication. At the same time, there is little doubt that the costs of selecting possibly relevant information have also risen rapidly. It is the well-known information paradox:

as information becomes cheaper and more information becomes available, the cost of selecting relevant information and of taking time to reflect, rises rapidly. For example, in the "old days" people used to sit down, compose a letter, put it in an envelope and send it off. This slow communication system made people think twice before sending something out, often reflecting and questioning the value of what they were saying. Some older people much prefer to communicate by letter than by phone. The fact that postal communication continued and still continues to exist for so long alongside telephone communication illustrates to some extent the many complementary – as opposed to purely substituting – characteristics of voice and written forms of communication.

Today, thanks to the ease of forwarding messages and sending them to multiple parties at once, little time for reflection is required, if not allowed for. Spontaneous, immediate near voice reaction has become the norm in email communication: speed and volume at the expense of content and reflection. These new features of electronic communication are clearly advantageous: they are more environmentally friendly (no paper required), "number" efficient (no need to write the same message over and over), and quick (unlike postal service messages, they can be sent and received almost immediately). However, there are negative aspects associated with the overflow and time wasted on identifying and selecting possible relevant information, which we would identify as a problem of "information pollution." A bit tax might help, to some extent, in reducing this information pollution.

In economic terms the use of marginal cost-pricing of common, network goods such as Internet services may lead to what has been called a "tragedy of commons" – a situation where a common resource is overutilized, causing unavoidable losses for society as a whole.[29] Economic theory teaches us that when confronted with such a negative externality, prices should exceed the marginal cost of production by the marginal social cost of congestion, reducing use of the resource to cases whereby the personal benefit to the consumer is greater than the social cost of usage. The bit tax, minute as it is, can be interpreted as an estimate of the marginal social cost of congestion. Levying a bit tax would, in other words, force users to focus their use of the Internet to activities with higher benefits than these marginal social costs.

Another area that might be positively affected by the bit tax is worker productivity. Some employers already complain that certain workers spend more time surfing the Net, sending personal emails or playing "addictive" computer games than actually doing their jobs. While there is a learning component to such addiction, there is also a significant cost. With all these tempting options at one's fingertips it is to some extent no wonder that people get distracted from their current work. Companies have had similar problems in the past with telephone usage, where employees could not resist the telephone and spent large amounts of time talking to friends or accessing third-party lines. Many companies have solved this problem by itemizing phone bills for each telephone extension within the organization, making employees pay for personal calls, blocking out third-party line access, and blocking out international phone line access. All of these initiatives have made employees more aware of their telephone usage. This, combined with the knowledge that they are being monitored, has curbed the desire to abuse privileges.

A similar issue was discussed in a recent article in which the cost to firms of Internet usage was addressed. The article begins by stating that many unnecessary and lengthy Internet searches will cost German industry over 100 million DM this year. According to a study by Pilot Software, a research agency based in Frankfurt, employees who have access to the Internet at their workplace spend over 7.5 hours per week surfing the Net. Gert Serwas, director of Pilot Software, states that the Internet offers inexhaustible information sources that "make the search time seem equally as inexhaustible."[30] He goes on to say that much of the information that even experienced users uncover can often simply be located by making one or two phone calls. Pilot Software concludes that clarity is more important than quantity, unlike industry leaders who believe that the best decisions are made based on the most amount of information possible. Again a bit tax, insofar as it would introduce a costing element in Internet use, could provide an incentive for more efficient use of electronic communication at work.

By way of conclusion: on possible uses of the bit tax

Naturally, there are plenty of suggestions for spending the revenues collected from the bit tax. The High Level Expert Group proposed the use of the tax as a means for financing the social security system in Europe. We will not extensively elaborate on this argument here.[31] However, we will say that at the outset this seems to be the most logical step, given the distributional implications of the new information and communication technologies and the challenges the emerging Information Society is putting to social cohesion policies, particularly in the European countries with highly developed but costly social welfare systems. On a priori grounds, the use of the additional bit tax revenues to fund, for instance, the employers' social security contributions in countries like Belgium, the Netherlands, France, Italy, or Germany should bring about a substantial reduction in labour costs, hence providing at least new incentives for job creation and improved competitiveness.

The impact of the bit tax on particular groups in society, sectors, or firms is something that remains very much an open issue and depends, as argued above, on the volume of tax revenues and the various responses by individuals and firms on a bit tax imposition. Obviously, the practical policy proposal should, as was also implicit in the High Level Expert Group report, be accompanied by measures that address the issue of IS "exclusion" and hence also possible exemption from a bit tax.

Under the heading of "universal service obligation," the expert group considered this issue when they recommended the need "to investigate in much greater detail whether in order to avoid exclusion and preserve regional cohesion, the current notion of 'universal service' should not be shifted in the direction of a notion of 'universal community service,' extending universal service provision to incorporate a basic level of access to new information services[32] but limited in its universality obligation to educational, cultural, medical, social, or economic institutions of local communities. Such a 'community' USP concept would in effect mean a return to the historical notion of 'universality' as introduced last Century in the U.S. with the advent of the telegraph. It would guarantee open access to the network and the carrier services and involve, where necessary, public funding for technical and financial assistance."[33] Such universal community service obligations would practically, by definition, imply various possibilities for bit tax exemption (hospitals, education establishments, etc.), as is common with VAT today.

A bit tax could also be instrumental in resolving the intellectual property rights problems associated with the networks. In the information age this issue has grown in importance as it has become increasingly difficult to compensate individuals and organizations for their work. Via the networks an individual can deliver perfect copies of digitized work to countless others, or upload a copy to a bulletin board or other service where thousands can download it or print hard copies.[34] This issue is of obvious importance for compensation, but also for network usage. Creators, publishers, and distributors of output may become, or are becoming, wary of the networks unless tools are developed that compensate them for their work. Thus, if intellectual property rights problems are not resolved, businesses, creators, and other owners of intellectual property rights could be discouraged from selling on-line, thus reducing network usage. Creators and other owners of intellectual property rights will not want to put their investments at risk. Since the bit tax would require usage to be itemized in some way, it could be developed to help collect intellectual property rights fees. The idea here is similar to the small tax that exists in many countries on photocopying, representing a common payment for foregone copyrights.

But this is certainly not the place to elaborate on the possible uses of something so speculative and controversial as a bit tax. The purpose of this discussion was to bring together some of the main arguments for why there is, at least in our view, an urgent need for investigating the feasibility of such a new tax notion. Our hope was not to detract the many "criticasters," but rather that those Internet users, communication experts, or policymakers who rejected the idea in an immediate, spontaneous, "cyber-like" fashion might reflect a little longer on some of the arguments presented here. The volume and the speed of the reactions received so far have not succeeded in convincing us that there is a strong argument for not investigating the issue.

Notes

1. See "Building the European Information Society for Us All, First Reflections of the High Level Group of Experts" (Interim Report produced for DGV Brussels, January 1996).
2. The idea of a "bit tax" was, as noted in the experts' group report, first put forward by Arthur Cordell and Thomas Ran Ide in "The New Wealth of Nations," a paper prepared for the Club of Rome, 30 November – 2 December 1994, now published as the second chapter of this book. A more elaborated version can be found in A. Cordell, "New Taxes for a New Economy," Government Information in Canada, vol 2, number 4, spring 1996.
3. Since August 1996, when this paper was first circulated and made available on the WWW, we have received no less than 200 emails reacting to the bit tax proposal. The publication of an article on the subject in Dutch newspapers (see further A.Groenhuis, "Belasting op Internet" ("Taxing the Internet"), NRC Handelsblad, 2 October 1996 and S. Stevens, "Internet en Belastingen" ("Internet and Taxes"), Weekblad 1996, 21 November 1996) has also served to increase interest in this extremely delicate issue. We are grateful for the many comments, often by outraged individuals, that we have received thus far.
4. As in the case of the Belgian Minister for Telecommunications Di Rupo at a conference on teleworking (see *Le Soir*, 6 June 1996).
5. The High Level Expert Group was chaired by Luc Soete.
6. See *Le Soir*, "Di Rupo, rêve d'une taxe sur les transferts de <bits> pour récolter 10 millards per an," 11 June 1996.
7. We are reminded of the story told by Nathan Rosenberg about the response of Faraday to the sceptical politician who asked Faraday

after he had discovered the basic principle of electricity (electromagnetic induction in 1831) what it was good for: "Sir, I do not know what it is good for. But of one thing I am quite certain, some day you will tax it." (Rosenberg, 1996).
8. See the official press release of the Flemish government: "Bit tax boort inspanningen van de Vlaamse regering de grond in" ("Bit tax undermines efforts of the Flemish government"), Brussels, 12 June 1996.
9. A good description but no solution of these challenges can be found in the EU's recent Green Paper "Living and Working in the Information Society: People First," 22 July 1996.
10. While there is a growing literature on Internet pricing and a lot of discussion on the Net of the advantages of "usage-based" versus the "flat rate" pricing (see J. MacKie-Mason and H. Varian, "Some FAQs about Usage-Based Pricing," September 1994, and Brody, "Internet@crossroads.$$$," *Technology Review*, May/June 1995), there has been very little written about alternative taxation systems on the Net.
11. Named after Robert Solow for his observation that "Everywhere around us we see computers except in the productivity statistics" (see "The OECD Jobs Strategy, Technology, Productivity and Job Creation," 1996).
12. See further statement by K.G. Abraham, Commissioner, Bureau of Labour Statistics before the Senate Finance Committee, 13 March 1995 and L. Nakamura, Federal Reserve Bank of Philadelphia, working paper no. 95-21, "Is U.S. Economic Performance Really That Bad?", October 1995.
13. See N. Newman, "The Great Internet Tax Drain," *Technology Review*, May/June 1996.
14. When *The Financial Times* is read on the Internet, the actual (physical) newspaper is not bought. The tax that would have been paid on the physical newspaper is "lost."
15. For further information see S. Gold, "AOL, CompuServe Sales Tax Looming in Europe" at: www.nbpacifica.com/daily/96.
16. See ISA State Taxation Task Force "Logging on to Cyberspace Tax Policy, Executive Summary" at http://www.isa.net/about/releases/taxexsum.html.

17. See "Selected Tax Policy Implications of Global Electronic Commerce," Department of the Treasury, Office of Tax Policy, 22 November 1996 at http://jya.com/taxpolicy.htm#6.
18. See K. Hart, "U.S. Touts duty-free Internet," *Communications Week International*, 26 November 1996.
19. See A. Cordell and T. Ran Ide, "The New Wealth of Nations."
20. That this is not an idea completely out of the clear blue sky idea is illustrated by the acknowledgement in the debate surrounding usage-based pricing that Internet use will have to become "metered, with users paying by the message, by the byte, or by the Web page, just as they now pay by the kilowatt-hour for electricity." H. Brody, "Internet@crossroads.$$$," *Technology Review*, May/June, 1995.
21. See Tobin's calculations in "Speculators' Tax" in *New Economy*. (Fort Worth, TX: The Dryden Press, 1994).
22. The argument of the Flemish government that "a 'bit tax' amounts to taxing the employment of the future in order to maintain employment of the past" is a good illustration of such exaggeration.
23. The billing and accounting costs of telephony is said to represent more than half what customers pay for a telephone call. However, as argued by MacKie-Mason and Varian ("Some FAQs about Usage-Based Pricing," September 1994), the main reason for this is the fact that marginal costs are "so low, not because billing costs are so large. Since it costs almost nothing to make a call during non-peak periods, accounting costs are almost 100% of the incremental cost of a non-peak call!" As a percentage of total costs, MacKie-Mason and Varian estimate AT&T's billing costs to be less than 10 per cent.
24. For further information see MacKie-Mason, "Pricing the Internet," a paper prepared for the conference on Public Access to the Internet, JFK School of Government, 26-27 May 1993; Gupta, Stahl and Whinston (1995), "Pricing of Services on the Internet," in *IMPACT: How ICC Research Affects Public Policy and Business Markets, A Volume in Honor of G. Kozmetsky*, Fred Phillips and W.W. Cooper (eds.), Quorum Books, CT and Stahl (1995). The paper by MacKie and Varian, "Some FAQs about Usage-Based Pricing," referred to above, contains a particularly useful overview of some of the advantages and disadvantages of usage-based pricing.

25. See again J. MacKie-Mason and H. Varian, op. cit.
26. See H. Brody, "Internet@crossroads.$$$."
27. Which we would identify as "distilled" knowledge, derived from experience of life, as well as from the natural and social sciences, from ethics and philosophy.
28. See "Building the European Information Society for Us All," page 3.
29. See further D. Stahl, "A Critical Survey of Internet Pricing Proposals," presented at the OECD conference on the economics of the information society, 30 November 1995.
30. Translated from Dutch to English: "Onnodig Internetten kost bedrijfswereld mijljoenen" ("Unnecessary use of Internet costs business community millions"), Belang Van Limburg, 28 October 1996.
31. For a more detailed argument on the employment aspects of the emerging information society, see Petit and Soete, "Employment in the Information Society: Analytical and Policy Challenges," a paper prepared as an analytical background report for the workshop on "The changing nature of employment" in support of the High Level Expert Group on the Information Society, Brussels, 9 September 1996.
32. This could be specified in functional rather than technical terms, such as possibilities for electronic networking, data and mail interchanges, access to new business, and information services available world wide and in core regions.
33. See "Building the European Information Society for Us All," page 43.
34. As Brody put it, "Want to mail a fund-raising appeal to 10,000 people? The Internet converts this from a $3,200 postal endeavour into one that's more or less on the house. Internet users seem to have found a kind of surreal restaurant where they can order a bottomless cup of coffee or a lobster dinner for 100 friends and no one ever presents an itemized bill." Op. cit., p. 1.